Pakistan's
Fourth Military Coup

Pakistan's
Fourth Military Coup

Edited by

Aftab Alam

Raj Publications

Delhi-110009 (INDIA)

First Published in 2001

ISBN 81-86208-15-1

Published by : **Raj Publications**
R-115/2, Model Town - III,
Delhi - 110009

Tel. : 7466486

Laser Typesetting by : Aarati Computers, Delhi-110 009

Printed at : Chawla Offset Printers, Delhi-110 052

PRINTED IN INDIA

Contents

Introduction

It was like a Hollywood thriller—plenty of suspense and action. Except that it was real. The story of the fourth military coup in Pakistan as pieced together from media reports, had all the ingredients of a hit movie. The coup d'etat of October 12, 1999 led by General Pervaiz Musharraf which displaced Sharif's civilian government was the reassertion of the military's dominant role in the polity after an interval of 11 years. The military this time, however, was able to wrest political power not because the top brass conspired to overthrow the civilian government. Rather, the inability of the political elite to manage the political crisis and the gradual erosion of civilian institutions encouraged the military once again to overthrow the civilian government which stood discredited by people because of its autocratic style of functioning.

The restoration of the democratic process after the death of General Zia in a misterious plane crash on August 17, 1988 witnessed the dismissal of four governments and the continuous fragility of political institutions. The period from 1988 to 1999 saw the holding of four general election, deepening of economic and political crises, and an upsurge of ethnic and sectarian strife. It was not a matter of surprise, therefore, when there was no political backlash against the suspension of the democratic process after the dismissal of the elected government of Prime Minister Nawaz Sharif on October 12. On the contrary, people expressed satisfaction when the army took control and reinstated the process of accountability. Pervaiz Musharraf, however, faced stiff and severe criticism from outside for the murder of nascent democracy in Pakistan.

It is not for the first time that Pakistan has experienced military rule. The first was in October 1958 when General Mohammad Ayub Khan imposed martial law and abrogated the constitution which the politicians had succeeded to make and implement after undergoing a hazardous constitution making journey of approximately nine years. The second time it was imposed by General Yahya Khan in March 1969, who tried to hold the state of Pakistan with the power of gun. The army intervened third time in 1977 under the leadership of General Zia to end the autocratic rule of Zulfikar Ali Bhutto. Infact, Pakistan most of the time since its inception as an independent state on August 14, 1947 has been under the military rule. Given the frequent spells of Martial Law and military's overt and subtle intervention in civilian afffairs, Pakistan is quite prone to the suspension of political process. It is not only military should be blamed for the destabilising democratic process, the responsibility, for the failure of democracy also lies with politicians, who in the garb of democracy worked most of the time in undemocratic and autocratic manner. The reign of Nawaz Sharif is a case in point.

The History of the military's interventions in Pakistan is long. However, there is a striking difference between this coup and the past ones. Unlike earlier coups which have been pro active, wherein the military sought political power, the present one only amounts to a reactive coup. In this case the military did not initiate matters but was clearly compelled to react to moves of the elected leadership which were aimed at destroying its institutional existence. Not only that, unlike the coups in past this time the army has not imposed martial law, banned political parties or unleashed a reign of terror against its political opponents. Nor has it imposed any restriction on the media.

The military coup in Pakistan did not happen overnight; grounds for the disintegration were being prepared all along. General Musharraf was merely a catalyst in that process of disintegration which has been relentlessly hurtling Pakistan towards chaos in recent years. Keeping in view the developments which were taking place, the coup was hardly unexpected. What was unexpected the timing. Paradoxically, the timing of the coup was not of the army's choosing. By sacking COAS General Pervaiz Musharraf, the civilian government forced the army's hand and precipitated a long impending clash between the government and military establishment. The talk of some kind of military intervention for restoring social, political and economic stability in the country had been in the air far over an year. A growing belief among an influential section of the intelligentia in Pakistan that solution to the horrendous problems and crises confronting the country could only be dealt by the army, had set the stage for a sure confrontation between the army and the civilian government.

Interestingly Prime Minister Nawaz Sharif himself is popularly perceived as having laid the ground for this coup as a result of his authoritarian approach to other democratic institutions. Instead of using his huge majority in the National Assembly to build a consensus within the country and leading Pakistan to a more prosperous and produtive future, he squandered a valuable opportunity in engoging himself in needless clash with other democratic institutions and the army. One find it hard to dispute Pervaiz Musharraf's contention that what he rolled back was not democracy, it was a sham. Nawaz Sharif had made sure that every political check on his freedom to do his will was effectively gotten out of the way--extraconstitutionally if necessary, and let the chips fall where they may. Instead of learning lessions from his first term, his second spell in office proved even more disastrous. During his tenure corruption and mismanagement were the order of the day, and the country was run as if it were a personal fiefdom.

Nawaz Sharif initiated a series of constitutional amendments to fortify himself against possible challenges to his rule and to invest himself with powers few constitutional rulers ever enjoyed. The first of his amendments dispensed with the President's power to dismiss a government and dissolve Parliament in a situation he thought was one of constitutional breakdown. That power had been written into the constitution by President Zia-ul-Haq, who had wished to retain with himself the ultimate leverage over the Prime Minister. The provision went on to cause the downfall of four elected governments in eight years. Nawaz Sharif's first government was one of the victims of this clause. This power, therefore, came to be regarded as a destabilising and undemocratic weapon in the hands of a head of state meant to be only a figurehead. For that reason, its repeal by Nawaz Sharif was generally welcomed. But there was more to come.

Nawaz Sharif's next amendment bonded parliamentary parties to the will of their party leader. It required every member to vote strictly in accordance with his or her party's (which meant party leader's) decision. Even abstention, let alone dissent, would cause the member to forfiet his or her seat. That had the effect of completely neutering the National Assembly. The opposition, being minuscule in the House turned into a pen of sheep. There was rarely a Parliament as dull as this one.

In his zeal to capture more and more power for himself he did not even distinguish between his friends and foes. He did not spare President Farooq Ahmad Leghari, who was his mentor and well wisher, and without whose covert and overt support he could not have managed his massive mandate at the hustings. President Leghari readily agreed to the passing of the 8th Amendment wherby he himself became a powerless figurehead. But he knew little about Nawaz Sharif's vengeful nature. Nawaz Sharif was inflamed when President Leghari supported the stand taken by then Chief Justice for probes into Nawaz Sharif's suspect financial dealings. Nawaz wanted Leghari out of his way to enable him to trample on all emaginary hurdles, and on the law whereby his own conduct could be questioned and investigated. Wanting to be above the law, he then simulteneously plotted the removal of Chief Justice Sajjad Ali Shah and went to the extent of okaying the disgraceful attack on the Supreme Court. It will be remembered as a most deplorable attempt by the head of the government to ridicule and deliberately humitiate the apex judiciary.

After denuding the President of his powers, subjugating the Parliament and humiliating the judiciary, this time Nawaz Sharif was out to conquer the army—the last and only institution that he thought, and rightly so, stood between him and his coronation. Infact Sharif had already made up his mind to clip the wings of the army at the first opportune time, when his first government was sacked by General Waheed Kakar. He was looking for right time. And after his successful forays against the President and the Judiciary, he thought that time had now come to trampel the army.

The departure of General Jehangir Karamat in October 98 was the initial manifestation of growing tension between the army and the political leadership. Nawaz Sharif successfully removed General Karamat simply because he respected the institution of chief executive constitution and cared about flourshing of nascent democracy. The only fault of General Karamat was his suggestion about a greater role of the army through establishing a national security council, in his address to the Naval Staff College at Lahore. General Karamat was a thorough professional, and was held in respect by rank and file of Pakistan army, and deserved to be appointed chairman JCSC. But instead he was retired under a well planted plot to debase the army. Sharif also tried to tinker with the institutional cohesiveness of the armed forces and to create ethnic rifts within their ranks in order to ensure the political loyality of important field commander. Then came his rash and impetuous decision to dismiss the Army Chief of Staff, General Pervaiz Musharraf while he was on a visit to Sri Lanka.

Sacking of General Pervaiz in midair and disallowing his aircraft to land at Karachi airport proves beyond doubt that hunger for absolute power had driven Sharif to insanity. Nawaz Sharif and his collaborators plotted the highjacking of PIA Airbus flight 805 with 200 passengers on board including General and Begum Pervaiz Musharraf and the air crew. Pk-805 was disallowed to land at Karachi and was ordered to divert to Nawabshah, he was reportedly told to land at Ahmedabad in India, and if that was not possible to ditch the aircraft in the sea. The aircraft was low on ful and the order imperitled the lives of the passengers. It was fortunate that with the help of PIA air crew General Musharraf managed to contact Lt. General Muzaffar H. Usmani, Corp

Commander Karachi, and apprised him of the siuation. Immediately Pakistani army came into action and took control of the airport and the plane eventually touched down at 6.50 pm with hardly any fuel left.

While this drama was being played out at Karachi, troops in Islamabad had put Sharif under virtual house arrest. A near clash occurred outside PTV headquarter when security forces, apparently police, tried to take back the control of the building from the army. Around 1820 hrs., the army headquarter sent additional troops led by a colonel to establish full control over the PTV building. But before they could do so, the news of General Musharraf's dismissal had been announced. At 2000 hrs., senior military commanders at army headquarter in Rawalpindi held consultations with General Musharraf in Karachi. The transmission from PTV and Radio Pakistan were restored by the army at 2215 hrs. Fifteen minutes later, PTV announced that the Sharif Government had been dismissed. General Musharraf stayed put in Karachi and even recorded his address to the nation there. He flew to Islamabad only in the early hours next day, just before his address to the nation went on the air at 0250 hours. By that time, the Pakistani army had taken complete control of the country. Sharif, who had secured a massive popular mandate less than three years ago, was a helpless prisoner in his mansion.

In his first televised address on 13th October 1999 General Musharraf accused Sharif's government of "septematically destroying" state institutions and driving the economy toward collapse. "You are all well aware of the kind of turmoil and uncertainty that our country has gone through in recent times..... I wish to inform you that the armed forces have moved in as a last resort to prevent further destabilisation". General Musharraf said in his speech. He also promised to announce his plans for Pakistan's future very soon.

Most interestingly, the action of the removal of the Nawaz government was received with relief right across the country. Given the massive unpopularity in the country that Nawaz Sharif managed to earn for himself in recent times, there was a widespread feeling of relief among the people which proved public disgust with the politicians. The Pakistanis would not be singing and dancing in the streets to celebrate the arrival of General Musharraf, but they were not shedding any tears on the departure of Nawaz Sharif either. The people of Pakistan did not necessarily approve of the military rule; they simply wanted to get rid of a civilian regime which they perceived as inept, corrupt, dishonest, insensitive and worst of all subservient to foreign interests.

Aware of the public sentiment against them, the Muslim League gave a muted response and qualified their protest by saying that they would not confront the army. What they did not say was that they had lost all public support. Not a voice was raised in Mian Nawaz Sharif's favour anywhere in the country. The eminent Journalist Najam Sethi, who not only welcomed military intervention but aso said that good government is more important than democracy at the present juncture, and that there should be no elections till the army cleanses the system. Against this backdrop, the rest of the world, which strongly condemned the coup and urged immediate restoration of democratic rule, is puzzled by the fact that Pakistani themselves do not seem to be overly worried about the toppling of a democratic regime in Islamabad.

After stabilising his full control over the country General Musharraf on October 17 unveiled a seven point agenda as a top priority for his government. He also attempted to give an account of the problems facing Pakistan. "There is dispondency and hopelessness surrounding is --- the slide has been gradual but has rapidly accelerated in the last many years. Today, we have reached a stage where our economy has crumbled, our credibility is lost, state institutions lie demolished; provincial disharmony has caused cracks in the Federation and people who were once brothers are now at each other's throat." "In sum", Musharraf said, "we have lost our honour, our dignity, our respect in the comity of nations. Is this the democracy our Quaid - e - Azam envisaged? Is this the way to enter the new millennium? --- Quite clearly, what Pakistan has experienced has been merely a lable of democracy, not the essence of it.... I shall not allow the people to be taken back to the era of sham democracy but to a true one."

The Chief Executive General Musharraf has laid down seven objectives for his regime—(1) rebuilding national confidence and morale; (2) strengthening the federation removing inter-provincial disharmony and restoring national cohesion; (3) reviving the economy and restoring investor confidence; (4) ensunring law and order and dispensing speedy justice; (5) de-politicising state institutions; (6) devolving power to the grassroots level and (7) ensuring swift and across the board accountability.

While announcing his agenda the Chief Executive refrained from giving a time frame for the restoration of democracy. Perhaps this move was deliberate and outcome of alot of thinking. His evasive and reluctant attitude for not giving a time frame could be understood keeping in view General Zia's promise of holding elections within 90 days which he did not fulfil and the multifaceted difficulties which the C.E. faced after assuming power. However the agenda laid down by the C.E. is leanthy and time consuming and no early return of democracy in Pakistan could be expected. The agenda aimed at achieving tangible political, social and economic results to the satisfaction of the people who because of development of events had been left in a lurch to look up to the army.

The new setup established by General Musharraf is described as "military rule sans martial law". For the first time in the history of Pakistan the army's takeover has not resulted in the imposition of martial law and the adoption of various punitive measure. This new experiment was necessary for a variety of reasons. The Chief Executive knew very well that the military rule for longer duration was unlikely to enjoy legitimacy and support in existing international environment. Whether we term the new setup as 'benign dictatorship' or with any other nomenclature, its survival depends upon its performance in terms of delivering concrete results to the people within the parameter of national agenda.

Having overthrown the Sharif's government, General Musharraf now faces the daunting task of rescuing the country from total collapse. The ground realities are very tough and challenges are formidable. There is need for fundamental reforms to root out corruption, give a vitality to the economy, recover the loot and restore the confidence and faith of general Pakistanis in the state. General Musharraf has set before him admirable objectives of cleansing up the monumental mess created by successive democratic governments and setting the house in order. The army has undertaken a great national responsibility of saving the country and returning towards a true democracy and good governance. But achieving there objectives may take a long time. In that case people may loose their paitence and anti-Sharif euphoria will fed away soon and this will be the real challenge before the General Musharraf. Thus he has to move decisively but with care and caution. General Musharraf in his address to the nation had said : "Our action will speak louder than words" and so they must indeed. People are fed up of endless rhetoric. Do not say it, do it, is the plea of millions of Pakistanis who want to see their country prosper and progress. They want promises backed by performance, result, not rhetoric. Most of all they want relief not redundancy.

1

Twelfth October and Beyond

**Wajahat Latif*

The 12th of October, 1999 will probably go down as the most dramatic day in the political history of Pakistan. At the Islamabad TV station, members of the elite force, a Nawaz Sharif personal protection group, and the soldiers of the army were the main characters of the drama. In the audience were press reporters including foreign correspondents, members of various diplomatic missions, TV personnel, technicians, peons, drivers, canteen staff and passersby. We don't know exactly what happened, but all agree that the prime minister's staff and the army major commanding the company deployed to takeover the TV station pulled ranks and then guns at each other.

At about the same time, in the skies over Karachi, a PIA flight from Colombo was being diverted to Nawabshah. Earlier, about 60 minutes after take off from Colombo, it was being diverted to Ahmedabad, India! As General Musharraf has now revealed himself, they were over Hyderabad on their way to Nawabshah that the GOC made contact with him to say that everything was now under control and so they could return to Karachi. With the fuel level falling dangerously, driven to the edge of his nerve, the pilot brought the aircraft back over Karachi. These must have been the scariest moments of his life. Such a highjacking was not known in aviation history. But he stayed calm and landed safely.

General Musharraf was cool, obviously, on account of his long experience as a commander. But the truly remarkable thing is that, in the tradition of the German army, his troops moved according to the will of their commander even though he was not present.

At a different venue in Islamabad, the Spanish National Day was being celebrated. The elegant Spanish ambassador was receiving her guests in the beautiful grounds of her residence. The news of the above drama had just broken and the atmosphere was charged with excitement. Rumours circulated freely. One was about an announcement from Lahore that martial law had been declared. The immediate reaction was "why from Lahore? The diplomatic corps, the mobile phones on their ears buzzing with messages from aides at the TV station and elsewhere in the city, were desperately trying to make sense of what had happened and mentally framing their despatches. A lady in sari raised her fist in the air, mock cheer leader fashion and shouted: "Nawaz is gone!"

By the next morning, we were all to learn that the Nawaz Sharif government had been removed and the armed forces were now in charge. The high drama was over. The "sham democracy" had left us. Roedad's prayer had been answered.

In Byron's words: "...truth is always strange/Stranger than fiction".

The action of the removal of the Nawaz government has been received with relief right across the country, from Khyber to Kashmir. The very few, including Asma Jehangir, who objected to the method, readily conceded the gross mismanagement and corruption of the Nawaz setup. The universal relief is proof of the public disgust with the politicians. Aware of the public sentiment against them, the Muslim League gave a muted response and qualified their protest by saying that they would not confront the Army. What they did not say was that they had lost all public support. Not a voice was raised in Mian Sahib's favour anywhere in the country. Several weeks and two observer delegations from abroad later, the situation remains the same.

Undoubtedly, the armed forces have an enormous amount of goodwill in the country at present to build upon. A bankrupt nation, used to living on doles and loans, corrupted to the core, is now hoping against hope that General Musharraf would pull them out from the bog where they find themselves dumped by the politicians.

Can Pervaiz Musharraf deliver?

First and foremost, the unity of command and discipline in the armed forces must remain intact. This is of the crucial importance if the general's plan of economic, political and moral reconstruction is to work. One has no doubt that this is uppermost in the chief executive's mind also. As far as possible troops should be kept out of the micro management of the state apparatus which should continue to be run by the civilians, being replaced by more efficient personnel where necessary.

Then, there are three obvious areas where the malady is rooted. The economy, especially the banking sector, the law and order and the foreign policy—all three have been devastated by extremely irresponsible and corrupt though elected government. Much will now depend on the team General Musharraf puts together to deal with the problems. He should look for people who have lived through the cancer of this country over the years and know what to do about it. They should be experts of the highest integrity on whon no finger can be raised. They should enjoy the complete trust of the government and have the freedom to work without interference. This fundamental change will show the improvement in the quality of governance very quickly.

No one believes, not the poor masses whom the general has promised a better life that these problems will go overnight. Everyone knows it is a long haul. But if the government is transparent and General Musharraf remains as sincere as he sounds now, the people will take the pressure of reform patiently.

Undoubtedly, the politicians will recover their breath and become cacophonous over the coming months. But this should not take the chief executive's mind off the objectives he set himself at the start and repeated in his press conference of the November 1. The people of Pakistan are not only enterprising and innovative but also generous and charitable. They have been denied a sincere and transparent leadership for a long time. Once they have it, the creativity of this nation will burst forth. They can do a lot with very little.

As a policy, the professionals should be given a free hand. It is possible that their plans take some time in implementation and might call for difficult decisions. But given their transparency and the public goodwill, people will support their actions.

Simultaneously and immediately, General Musharraf must whip up massive municipal activity and implement public impact projects. People remember Azam Khan's martial law in Lahore for the municipal work it did. Streets were cleaned, rubbish disposal, hygiene standards in public places improved. Every city today needs such cleaning up. The issue of slums and ghettoes should be addressed through civil society collaboration and government support where necessary.

Management of traffic on roads and highways is another immediate need. This is not a difficult task. The existing legislation on the subject is copious and effective, provided there is will to enforce the law. There are outstanding officers serving in the ranks of the police and traffic engineers who will be ready and able to deliver. Horns fitted in motor vehicles, particularly pressure horns are a major source of noise pollution. The use of pressure horns is illegal but so common that even government vehicles, schools busses and vans have them.

Public transport needs to be improved and regulated. The emphasis should shift from costly road construction projects to intelligent traffic management and law enforcement. There is also an urgent need to attend to encroachments on roads and pathways. A major campaign to eliminate them should be undertaken. Encroachments on public land and forceful dispossessions of the poor farmers by the strong and the powerful has led to a culture of lawlessness which must be changed.

In themselves these are no earthshaking reforms but they introduce visible order in society and make life bearable. As they are related to daily life of all citizens, such actions have great public impact.

In conclusion, the people do not expect miracles. They are used to a hard life and know that the problems are chronic. But what they do wish to see is that those now in the driving seat have a good sense of direction. That, simply, is the difference between hope and despair.

---

* Courtesy : *The Pakistan Times,* November, 21,1999

2

Nawaz Sharif's Failed Coup

** Air Marshal (Retd), Ayaz Ahmed Khan*

Nawaz Sharif is likely to be remembered as an unwise head of government, who frittered away many opportunities of good governance during his two tenures and was forced out of office by self-made crisis and plots. In November 1990 Nawaz Sharif became prime minister after winning an election during which he had the "moral support" of then President Ghulam Ishaq Khan and General Mirza Aslam Beg, then Chief of the Army Staff at the time. He was sailing along quite well till he unwisely decided to do the unexpected ie confront the president. He conspired to get rid of President Ghulam Ishaq Khan who had helped bring him into power. This unwise move brought his first tenure to an abrupt end in mid term. He was removed from office on April 11, 1993. He became victim of his bellicosity and seized by ulterior motives planned to sack an experienced head of state. He was doing well, and so was the country, but suddenly became disrespectful towards the president who had demanded transparency in financial dealings, and had objected to the misuse of state funds, especially forcing banks to give huge loans to his cronies.

It was Nawaz Sharif's doing that he and President Ghulam Ishaq Khan were removed from office unceremoniously by then Chief of the Army Staff General Abdul Waheed Kakar. Had Nawaz

Sharif been an intelligent and a mature person, he would have completed his first tenure successfully. And that would have been good for Pakistan. He undid his own self and harmed the country.

During his second tenure which started in February 1997, he plotted the removal from office of President Sardar Farooq Ahmed Khan Leghari who was his mentor and well wisher, and without whose overt and covert help he could not have managed his massive mandate at the hustings. Farooq Leghari as president had readily agreed to the passing of the 8th Amendment whereby he became a powerless figurehead. But he knew little about Nawaz Sharif's vengeful nature. Nawaz Sharif was inflamed when Leghari supported the stand taken by then chief justice for probes into Nawaz Sharif's suspect financial dealings. Nawaz wanted Leghari out of his way to enable him to trample on all imaginary hurdles, and on the law whereby his own conduct could be questioned and investigated. Wanting to be above the law, he then simultaneously plotted the removal of Chief Justice Sajjad Ali Shah, and went to the extent of okaying the disgraceful attack on the Supreme Court. That shameful assault by a vulgar mob led by Mushahid Hussain and Tariq Aziz MNA was at the behest of Nawaz Sharif. If will be remembered as a most deplorable attempt by the head of the government to ridicule and deliberately humiliate the apex judiciary. It is a permanent stigma on the face of the Pakistani nation.

Having been sacked by the Chief of the Army Staff-General Waheed Kakar in the midst of his first tenure, Nawaz Sharif had made up his mind to clip the wings of the army at the first opportunity. He assigned the defence portfolio to himself more for containing the army than doing any good to it. He reluctantly tolerated General Jehangir Karamat who was an appointee of President Sardar Farooq Khan Leghari. General Karamat's good reputation and popularity in the army tormented him. He specifically appointed retired Lt. General Iftikhar Ali Khan, brother of Chaudhry Nisar Ali Khan to keep a close watch on the army especially on COAS General Jehangir Karamat.

The suggestion of General Jehangir Karamat in his address to the Naval Staff College at Lahore for a national security council provoked Nawaz Sharif into demanding his immediate resignation. General Jehangir Karamat was a thorough professional, and was held in great respect by the rank and file of Pakistan Army. Had Nawaz Sharif been a wise and a mature leader, he would not have overlooked the academic suggestion put forward by the COAS. Apparently Defence Secretary Lt Gen Iftikhar Ali sided with and stoked prime minister's excitement over the event and forced the COAS into pre-mature retirement.

Being the senior most among the three Service Chiefs General Jehangir Karamat should have been allowed to continue his tenure; and deserved to be appointed as Chairman Joint Chiefs of Staff Committee. But the smallminded Nawaz Sharif had an unforgiving nature. His ego could not be satisfied without humiliating the highly respected Pakistani Army chief in full glare of national and world media. His real motive was to put the army in its place by debasing the dignity of its chief.

Nawaz Sharif's coup against General Pervaiz Musharraf and for that matter against Pakistan Army took shape on July 4, 1999, when he willingly submitted to President Bill Clinton's diktat to force Kashmiri Mujahideen out of the Drass-Kargil mountain tops. By so doing, Nawaz Sharif rescued the Indian Army from impending defeat and disaster. It is well known that the Indian Army was in serious trouble in Drass, Kargil and Batalik areas. It had suffered very high casualties. Thousands of Indian troops were killed and thousands were without rations, supplies and proper clothing in the battle areas and even in Siachin. Prime Minister Atal Behari Vajpayee in desperation had telephoned Bill Clinton and informed him of the plight of Indian troops. He had appealed to Bill Clinton to rescue India from disaster at the hands of Kashmiri Mujahideen. He told him of the consequences of such a defeat. Vajpayee asked Clinton to pressure Nawaz Sharif to remove the "Islamic terrorists" ie Kashmiri Mujahideen from the mountain tops in the Kargil sector. Clinton wanted to cash on this opportunity to oblige India, and belittle the Mujahideen and Pakistan Army, and thereby further American interests in South Asia.

Nawaz Sharif's readiness to become an American-Indian tool on Washington's diktat without national consensus or approval of the Parliament, turned an imminent defeat into victory for India, and Pakistan's victory on the ground into a diplomatic defeat. Had he possessed grit, vision and courage, he would have rejected US pressure, and would have directed Pakistan Army and the PAF to go to the help of the Kashmiri freedom forces to consolidate their hold on the 166 mountain tops and cut off Kargil, Siachin and Ladakh by blocking Srinagar Kargil highway. Nawaz Sharif just succumbed and gave in to the utter disappointment of the Pakistani nation.

The BJP drummed up and gained immense propaganda value and in fact BJP's success at the polls was made possible by the withdrawal forced on the Mujahideen by Mian Nawaz Sharif. Sensing national despair and disappointment, he tried to make a scapegoat of the army leadership. He alleged that he was not informed and was kept in the dark about the deployment and the scope of Kargil operations. He was telling a lie. General Pervaiz Musharraf made it public that the prime minister was kept fully informed throughout. As a professional soldier General Pervaiz reiterated that a victory was won, and India was humbled.

While avoiding an open row with the army, Nawaz Sharif on the advice of Shahbaz Sharif and Lt General Khwāja Ziauddin decided to act against the COAS at an opportune time. These two bedfellows cooked up the lie that the army was planning to overthrow the elected government. They were up to a lot of mischief during their Washington visit and it is felt that the plot hatched by the above two gentlemen with the knowledge of the prime minister was leaked to the US Administration. By edging out the incumbent COAS by a junior Lt. General of Corps of Engineers, the real motive was to weaken the army by creating discord in its ranks. This would have pleased Pakistan's enemies, especially India.

The dangerous drama was being staged to gain US support that an impending military takeover was crushed.

Another motive behind the Nawaz-Ziauddin plot was to divert public attention and resentment from the messy and chaotic political and economic situation. It has now transpired that Nawaz Sharif had hatched a conspiracy in connivance with Lt. Generals Tariq Pervaiz, Ziauddin and Brigadier Javed Malik. A military inquiry into the matter would soon reveal the whole truth. The coup attempt failed because the above three officers were black sheep in the otherwise highly disciplined and professional Pakistan Army.

That Nawaz Sharif got involved in the coup attempt against the Chief of the Army Staff who was his own appointee and who was recently appointed by him as Chairman Joint Chiefs of Staff Committee is astonishing. It just shows that the man is brainless. He totally disregarded General Musharraf's high professionalism, patriotism, integrity and loyalty to the state and to the head of the government ie to Nawaz Sharif as prime minister. An ordinary Pakistani citizen could vouch and testify without reservation that Pakistan Army under the command of General Pervaiz Musharraf could never think of a coup against an elected government. Whether Nawaz Sharif fell in the trap laid by Lt. General Tariq Pervaiz, Lt. General Khwaja Ziauddin, Brigadier Javed Malik and their accomplices, or this was his own brain child, would be soon established by the Military Inquiry Committee.

Nawaz Sharif has once again proved that he does not use his brain or logic, and goes by whims, and has proved to be fickle to the extreme. He is guilty of collaborating with betrayers and renegades, because he has tried to divide and damage Pakistan Army. He should have demanded proof from the collaborators and subverts before resorting to the deplorable and unlawful action in firing the army chief when he was returning from Sri Lanka, and was in mid air. By disallowing his aircraft to land at Karachi, Nawaz Sharif and his collaborators endangered the life of General Pervaiz Musharraf and other passengers.

That Nawaz Sharif could steep so low is distressing and frightening. Nawaz Sharif will pay the price for his follies, especially for the failed coup that he stage-managed and mismanaged. Pakistan cannot afford such charades, because it is the country and the people of Pakistan who suffer in the end for the wickedness of our rulers.

---

* Courtesy : *The Frontier Post (Pakistan)*, October 21, 1999.

3

Ouster of the 'Prime Monster'

** Tarique Niazi*

Think of a prime minister who orders his henchmen to let a Pakistan International Airlines jet — with 200 passengers, mostly Pakistanis, on board - burn out its fuel until it tumbles out of the sky to meet its infernal death on ground. Why? Because he wants one of the passengers, his Chief of Army Staff, kept off the ground, dead or alive, for two hours necessary to complete the conspiracy of his overthrow. To make it happen, he already bought off three generals — two corps commanders and the Chief of the Inter Services Intelligence (ISI), turned them into rats to snitch on their chief, beat them into a "stab-in-the-back," and launched them on to his "death mission." These generals together with the prime minister's civilian underlings, hired the PIA chief, civil aviators, Sindh Police chief, Sindh administration chief, and a clutch of "uniformed creeps" from the ranks of their service as would-be assassins to make a funeral pyre of 200 airborne travellers.

When the plane approached the Karachi airport for landing, two hours had already gone by. By then the conspirators in the Prime Minister's House had lost their battle. Their pursuers, hot on their trail, had already thrown a ring around their mansion—the Prime Minister's House—and their amplifier, Pakistan

Television - from which they were conspiring to blow up 200 human lives, most of whom, indeed, work hard to keep those who now turned out to be conspirators in their mansions. And all that was accomplished long before the Chief of Staff could even set his foot on the soil of Pakistan. If he was eliminated in the process, there were heavy odds of a civil war.

Nawaz Sharif, as an accomplished conspirator, laid a trap for his COAS, whom he reappointed on September 30 to the twin command of Pakistan Army and the Joint Chiefs of Staff for another two years. Weeks after, he sent him to Colombo, Sri Lanka, to represent his government at the Lankans' fifty years of independence celebrations. Within hours of the COAS's scheduled return home, Nawaz Sharif and his allied conspirators struck. A brief statement of the firing of the chief and hiring of his replacement flashed across television screens all across the country. With this, a civilian coup against the military leadership was complete. For that brief moment, Pakistan armed forces were turned into Nawaz's "rent-a-cop security enterprise."

In this conspiracy, Nawaz lived up to his past pattern of deceit that had ensnared former Chief Justice Sajjad Ali Shah. Through Pakistan's embassy in Riyadh, Nawaz wangled an invitation from a phantom group of "concerned Pakistanis" there for Justice Shah to speak to them. A former chief justice, a former bureaucrat, and a serving journalist were made part of this grand set-up. Justice Shah swallowed the bait and went off to meet with his "concerned" audience in the October of that year, only to discover that he was standing before a bunch of "Nawaz loyalists." They were corralled by the embassy to talk back at the Shah for his Supreme Court's "judicial activism" that was, as per their script, hobbling a "democratic government." Back home, the conspiracy against Justice Shah was all but complete. His brother judges had been successfully prodded to turn on and against him. A full court was scheduled to be held without the chief justice in intimation. When Justice Shah was reported the coup, he, like the COAS, rushed back home, and soon after landing in Karachi ordered his registrar to rewrite the docket. Yet conspirators were successful in tearing down the Supreme Court into four splinters—one each landing at Quetta, Peshawar, Lahore, and Karachi—to turn against its principal seat in Islamabad. All that wound up in the sad departure of Justice Shah, and an ever-weakened faith in the nation's highest court, an outcome Nawaz Sharif long awaited to savor.

Since February 1997, when he began his term as prime minister, Nawaz fired four service chiefs who refused to have a "price tag" on them. This led him to play divisive politics to sow discord among the services, and disintegrate their unity of command. This past year he had all but promoted Iftikhar Ali, brother of a federal minister, to a rank of four-star general—a rank parallel to that of the then COAS Gen. Jehangir Karamat. Gen. Karamat aborted the move by firing Gen. Iftikhar Ali. In subversive retaliation, Nawaz took the fired general under his wings and appointed him defence secretary to oversee all three services—army, navy, and airforce. Indeed, a slap in the face of Gen. Karamat, and more so a diabolic move to crack up the armed forces. Later, Iftikhar Ali co-led the post-Kargil defamation campaign that made martyr of Nawaz and a "rogue" of the army.

In his first term (1990-1993) as prime minister, Nawaz opened war with his COAS Gen. Asif Nawaz, after the latter refused to succumb to his moneyed temptations. Nawaz then moved in on the less-resistant corps commanders to buy them off. Gen. Asif Nawaz, as it is now documented, solemnly accused Nawaz of buying off his corps commanders and splitting their loyalties against their lawful command. This is when Gen. Asif Nawaz's corps commanders came to be known as "Crore Commanders".

In line with his past tradition, Nawaz, in his second term, again attempted to seed the army with the corrupt influence of money. He successfully bought off two corps commanders, Gens. Saleem Haider and Tariq Pervez, who sided with Nawaz to give him pass on the "botched Kargil offensive" and instead blame it on their COAS. Later these generals together with Nawaz's ISI chief, Gen. Ziauddin provided grist to the rumour mills of a "possible coup" by the COAS, Gen. Musharraf.

Were Nawaz not an ethically rotten man, whose self-interest always trumped the national interest, he would own up to the Kargil offensive that he himself approved to its zero-ground. Ironically or demonically, he green-lighted the offensive at the same time he was signing a "peace accord" with Indian Prime Minister A.B. Vajpayee during his visit this year to Lahore. When the generals pointed out to his contradictory behaviour of signing the peace and scheming the offensive at once, Nawaz, *Dawn* reported, replied: "You do your job; I shall do mine." Fine! Then generals did their job by doing Nawaz's bidding in Kargil. When it was Nawaz's turn to do his, he disarmed the generals and threw them to the wolves to be savaged and paraded as "rogues". When the nation cried foul to see the armed forces brutalised as "rogues" it deserted Nawaz en mass. On September 1, Nawaz's hometown, Lahore, was drowned with the shouts of "Down with the Sharifs." Two days after, the whole country was shut down to show its disgust at the Sharifs. Dismayed, he rushed his brother and his ISI chief to Washington to squeal on a "phantom fundamentalism" in the army that was about to topple him to punish his peace offensive in Kargil, his planned crackdown on religious extremism, and his attempts to take on the Taliban.

Since his removal on October 12, to this day of October 18, not a single sectarian killing has been reported anywhere in the country. This quiet raises the question: Who was behind the Shites' massacre? Prime Minister? His co-conspirators? To convince Washington of religious extremism? These questions need be answered-after a thorough probe. On the Taliban, Nawaz was equally savage. Since last year, he has been hopscotching the country to pitch for the Taliban's "criminal justice system" as a model for Pakistan to follow. This hawking of his finally led him to have the National Assembly—the lower house of 237 members where Nawaz's Muslim League commands two-thirds majority—passed the 15th Constitutional Amendment that is a replica of the Taliban's criminal justice system, frequently swaddled as the "Shariat Law." Ever since the passage of this amendment by the National Assembly, Nawaz Sharif had pulled out every stop to get it passed in the Senate also, where it ran into snags because of the powerful opposition. Today, Pakistanis wonder: Was Mian Mohammad Nawaz Sharif a prime minister or a prime monster?

Moral: Seniority should be made the sole governing principle for future appointments of service chiefs and their command at Joint Chiefs of Staff. This principle has threefold advantages: First, it will eliminate subversive incentives for civilian leadership to hunt favorites in the armed forces and thus cause split within and among them. Second, it will keep ambitious commanders from ingratiating themselves with civilian bosses, over and above the heads of their service chiefs, for rewards in money or senior appointments. Third, it will do away with the imagined or real threats of mutual interference by civilian and military leaders in their respective domains. Just as the "seniority" principle has realised all three advantages in the appointments of Supreme Court chief justices, it is sure to work these advantages for the armed forces and their "democratic leaders" as well.

---

* Courtesy : *The Frontier Post (Pakistan),* October 21, 1999.

4

Nawaz's Fall from Grace

** M.S. Qazi*

The drop scene of the Machiavellian move engineered by the deposed prime minister Nawaz Sharif to show the door to chairman JCSC and COAS, General Pervaiz Musharraf ended in dramatic events of October 12 and his steep fall from the high office. This development temporarily relieved the nation from tension-ridden crises which had pushed the country towards uncertainty through a highly destabilised situation and strong rumour-mongering. But, the story does not end here; in fact it only just started. Let's analyse the reason for Nawaz Sharif' fall from grace, why things went wrong and what lies ahead for us as a nation.

During the ensuing period of confrontation between the prime minister and COAS from July 4 to October 12, Nawaz Sharif acted a directionless cliffhanger. Buoyed up by his previous phony successes, he was over-confident whereas he should have treaded carefully. He had earlier sent a CJ of Pakistan home with the connivance of some members of the apex court and covert support of outsiders who played the role of 'insiders' and sent plummeting the prestige, integrity and credibility of the apex court. He sent previous COAS home simply because he respected the institution of chief executive, constitution and cared about flourishing of nascent democracy. His personal commitment to democracy was construed to be his weakness in the background of role of the army in national politics in the past and its responsibility to safeguard national integrity and internal security whenever political direction went haywire.

Nawaz Sharif successfully reprimanded and expelled any member of his ruling party who had the audacity to create fissure in party against his authoritative, secretive, hasty and erratic decisions. He succeeded to dump parliamentarians as a heap of ineffective elected representatives and decorated presidency with a loyalist who would only utter sentences of total loyalty to Nawaz Sharif. Yet his love and craving for absolute power which he wanted through the 15th Constitutional amendment, had no limits. To satisfy his appetite for power he enjoyed staying on the edge of precipice without being mindful that a free fall from there could hurt the nation more than him. On October 12, he had the fall and must have tasted its bitter effects but this has left the nation in a lurch.

Article 58 2(b) of the Constitution, a legacy of Gen. Zia, had constitutionally empowered the president of Pakistan to be final arbiter to decide the fate of an elected government during any political crises. He could dismiss a government. In fact between 1988 to 1997 four elected governments were dismissed by three presidents. Nawaz Sharif's government was one of the three governments which were previously dismissed. Nawaz Sharif's first act after becoming a prime minister for the second time in 1997 was to do away with Article 58 2(b) of the constitution because of more than two-thirds majority he enjoyed till he was deposed. With the disappearance of Article 58 2(b) authoritative control over parliamentarians because of 14th amendment to the constitution, state power converged in the hands of Nawaz Sharif rather than in the state institutions. Removal of the chief justice in 1998 through legally dubious means was one of the acts to empower the chief executive at the cost of judiciary. This time Nawaz Sharif wanted to empower himself at the expense of army.

An obvious and inescapable consequence of concentration of power in the hands of chief executive was that it made the prime minister politically unaccountable for his acts of commission and omission even on sensitive issues of national security and poor performance of his government.

The Kargil conflict ended on a negative note with three implications, one each for the army, Nawaz Sharif and the Kashmir issue. The army valued tactical gains made on the high mountains of Kargil with the support of Kashmiri Mujahideen and looked up to the prime minister to use tactical military gains as a bargaining chip to extract something tangible from the Indians on the Kashmir issue. That was the perception that existed amongst the people of Pakistanis as well.

Nawaz Sharif and his diplomatic team led by Sartaj Aziz could not deliver the results. Instead Nawaz Sharif rushed to Washington and settled for "humiliating" withdrawal of troops from Kargil on President Clinton's assurance of taking "personal interest" in getting the Kashmir issue resolved. The Army's rank and file could not take such a decision kindly. The nation also considered withdrawal of troops a national humiliation and a direct insult to the sacrifices made by army personnal and the mujahideen. Nawaz Sharif certainly wanted the COAS to accept the responsibility of Kargil conflict and quit. He, unlike, General Karamat did not oblige him.

Nawaz Sharif felt insecure and looked towards Washington for a bail-out. He feared that he would be eased out of office by the army. Statement by an unknown official of the state department that the US would not welcome change of government in Islamabad through "extra-constitutional" means did put army high command in somewhat embarrassing situation. They were not planning removal of the prime minister through extra-constitution means despite their differences with him on the Kargil issue.

Nawaz Sharif's bid to seek Washington's overt support to stay in power was because of the negative fallout of the Kargil conflict, opposition at home by religious and political parties, humiliating surrender in Washington July 4, unpopularity which his government had earned because of poor governance, sectarian violence and ill conceived economic policy which over past 32 months had further deteriorated the state of economy instead of improving it and made IMF's hold on national economy total and complete. His only option was to exercise absolute power to crush any opposition which could not be possible without politicising the army and making it subservient to his whimsical style of governance. It was least acceptable to the army as an institution.

Appointment of former ISI chief, Lt. Gen. Ziauddin as COAS was a step in that direction, other wise appointment of COAS, a week earlier to the dual charge of CJCSC had clearly indicated to the public that Nawaz Sharif had settled down to work with COAS. It was a Machiavellian move on his part to fulfil his ambition. He wanted to remove COAS unceremoniously as the events on October 12 unfolded. The army as an institution could not accept its politicisation and disgraceful exit of its COAS after General Karamat. It acted unitedly to safeguard itself against the undesirable acts of a political maverick.

It is to be appreciated that supremacy of the civilian authority over military establishment enshrined in the constitution of Pakistan becomes credible only if the civilian government functions and takes decisions pertaining to national security and on matters of national importance through a well established democratic process. Decision making during 32 months rule of Nawaz Sharif clearly indicated that he was averse to strengthening democratic institutions and preferred to take personal decisions on matters of national importance and trusted no one except his brother, the former CM of the Punjab.

Nawaz Sharif treated the state of Pakistan as a family affair. His style of governance was an recipe to foment crisis every now and then. His policies pushed the army to assert herself in larger national interest. The drop scene of October 12 events can be clearly visualised and justified in such a background. No one protested against the removal of Nawaz Sharif. It lend credence to the general belief that his government had lost public support and even the support of PML parliamentarians.

Despite his unpopularity and authoritative rule his removal from the office has precipitated constitutional crisis in the country. Martial Law is no solution to the crises faced by the country. A return to rule of law and democracy should be the first and foremost national priority, whatever way is carved to get out of the post-military takeover situation. The constitution, if necessary, should be amended to ensure that despots like Nawaz Sharif in future do not fiddle with state institutions and democratic process in the country.

The government of deposed prime minister and the previous governments remained irresolute to address the problems arising out of massive corruption, unemployment and inefficiency in government departments, public enterprises and financial institutions. Consequently the economy remained hostage to ill-conceived policies and during past six months did not show any tangible sign of turning around despite revival of ESAF/EFF by the IMF. Therefore, putting economy back on track, cleansing the society of corruption and making civil administration efficient should be the second national priority.

Keeping in view concentration of state power in Nawaz Sharif's hands, his erratic and personalised style of governance which scuttled growth of democracy in the country, his fiddling with the democratic institutions and making them dysfunctional, politicising the army—only to make personal gains and to acquire unlimited powers justified intervention by the army albeit for short time to restore order and stability in the country. It was essential to safeguard country's internal security. The army has full support of the people for this 'limited mandate'. Going beyond that would not be in the national interest.

---

* Courtesy : *The Frontier Post (Pakistan),* October 18, 1999

5

Deposition of a King-to-be

** Ashraf Ali Chaudhry*

"*Ruin comes when a trader, whose heart is lifted up by wealth, becomes ruler.*"- Plato

After denuding the president of his powers, subjugating the Parliament, taming the bureaucracy and humiliating the judiciary through his most shameful attack on the apex court, this time around the king to be was out to conquer the army—the last and the only institution that he thought, and rightly so, stood between him and his coronation.

Nawaz Sharif's past successful forays against the president, the Parliament, the bureaucracy, and the judiciary had emboldened him to such an extent that he had the least hesitation in launching his assault on this last institution firstly by forcing the retirement of one army chief and then by sacking the other while he was still airborne.

It would have been a matter of no consequence to him if in this attempt, the plane carrying the army chief had crash-landed, killing all on board including the General and his 200-plus fellow-travellers.

While most of the newspaper comments have so far focussed on the post-Oct. 12 developments offering their recipes for the future of this unfortunate country, few have tried to visualise the scenario that would have emerged in case this firstever coup by a sitting prime minister of a country against his own army had succeeded. The PTV would have immediately flashed a "breaking news" headline informing the Pakistanis that the plane carrying the army chief and 200 others had crashed in mid-air due to some technical fault; the search is on to find the black box to determine the exact cause of the accident; a high-powered civil and military team has been formed to conduct the investigation and submit its report to the PM within 48 hours. The mortal remains, if any, of the army chief would have been buried with full military honours at his ancestral place. A cash award would have been announced by the PIA for all those killed and injured in the accident. A day after, the PM and other dignitaries would have been shown with very morose and gloomy looks on their faces on the TV as well as in the newspaper pictures, visiting the "late General's" residence offering their condolences to the bereaved family. The PM on this occasion would also have very graciously made, though for media consumption only, some offer of an apparently a very lucrative job to Bilal Musharraf.

All these rituals would have been over in a day or two and thereafter every thing in the country would have gone 'royal'—the Royal Pakistan Army, the Royal Pakistan Air Force, the Royal Pakistan Navy, the Royal Pakistan Air Lines and so on. The Commonwealth instead of suspending our membership would have rather celebrated the elevation of one of its members to the royal status. Our relations with the IMF, World Bank and the greatest "champion" of democracy, the sole superpower—the United States—would have become most cordial as our emissaries would always have been on their toes to go wagging their tails wherever these Masters had liked them to go, to sign whatever papers they wanted them to sign, be it in the Blair House or on the pavement outside it. That perhaps also explains as to why the West is currently feeling so concerned over the deposition of our king to be, who in their eyes was the only democrat this side of the Suez.

In addition to the above, there would also have been many other advantages. Like the British Queeen Mother, we would also have a King Father ensconced in the royal palaces of Raiwind. The media would have gone mad in projecting Hussain Nawaz and Hussan Nawaz as heir-apparents. The media would also have tries to flatter the ordinary people for their overnight transformation from being the citizens of a poor, under developed country of the Third World to those of the Royal Kingdom of Pakistan. In actual practice though, the changeover would have meant for them little else than the imposition of a few more royal taxes and some further rise in the prices of essential items as more of these would have been required for the Royal kitchen. "His Majesty" would also have taken pains during his public appearances to exhort his loyal subjects to work still harder to fill the royal coffers without bathering about their own bread and butter, this being the normal standard behaviour of the subjects of all kingdoms.

In due course of time, the country and its people would have adjusted themselves to the new system and lived 'peacefully' ever after because the kings do not at all allow anybody to disturb their peace.

'Unfortunately' however, General Pervaiz Musharraf and his Rawalpindi Corps Commander turned out to be great spoilsports despite having been caught unawares. What however puzzles most observers is that what other qualities, if any, could General Ziauddin Butt boast of except his Kashmiri clout with the deposed prime minister. One simply shudders to imagine as to what would have happened to the Pakistan Army if it had unfortunately come under the command of a person of Ziauddin's calibre and character.

Now that the Providence has placed the responsibility of shaping the destiny of this nation on the shoulders of General Pervaiz Musharraf, the world in general and the Pakistanis in particular are watching his each and every move very carefully. The standard practice of all new entrants to the corridors of power in the past has been to start modestly by projecting themselves as ones not interested in power but simply in cleansing the proverbial Augean stables.

However in due course of time those around them succeed in convincing them about their indispensability for the country. Soon they themselves also start enjoying the trappings of power. They forget their declared agenda and start focussing mainly on keeping themselves in the saddle. All that they do for public amusement is that they bring in some new faces to the top echelons of power and reshuffle the bureaucracy to create an impression that much is happening or is about to happen. But once the dust has settled down, things remain where they were or in some cases become even worse.

Leaving aside the personal ambitions, if any, of the new set of rulers, there are also some genuine impediments in the way of changing the status quo. People who are patriotic, upright and also competent enough to implement the revolutionary agenda effectively, are really a very rare commodity and hence are hard to find. Secondly, the traditional ruling elite have spread their tentacles in all spheres of our national life in such a way that nothing can move without their consent and co-operation. The pressure exerted by the foreign powers who are obviously motivated by their own self interests, makes the situation all the more complicated. However let us hope that this time our new rulers are able to rise to the occasion to find ways and means to bring about a really healthy and positive change in our system of governance.

In doing, so, they should be misled neither by the hypocritical foreign promptings for the early restoration of the so-called sham democracy nor by the incessant internal chorus for speedy accountability and early return to the barracks, being sung by the politically active and vocal elements.

What is really imperative for the wielders of power in this country is to realise that their primary and foremost duty and responsibility is to safeguard the rights and interests of the silent majority which have continued to be ruthlessly trampled and flagrantly violated by successive regimes despite much lip-service.

While the elections and the sham democracy, of which we have had enough experience in the past, may be of great interest to our traditional ruling elite comprising the feudal lords and the urban upper crust as they have nothing else to do, the silent majority is least interested in such luxuries. What they are interested in is only and only good governance irrespective of the fact as to who provides it and how provides it. They strongly believe in the age old maxim of political science. "For forms of government, let the fools contest. Whatever is governed best, is best."

Until and unless the rulers are able to provide some relief to the downtrodden of this country whom the past regimes have been crushing under the weight of innumerable direct and indirect taxes and spiralling inflation, the accountability and restoration of sham democracy will remain totally meaningless and immaterial thereby paving the way for a revolution which, God forbid, could be bloody.

Postscript: When Plato said "Ruin comes when a trader whose heart is lifted up by wealth becomes ruler", he also added "or when the General uses his army to establish a military dictatorship".

---

*Courtesy : *The Frontier Post,* November 2, 1999.

6

Pakistani Roulette

* *Mubarik Shah*

Pakistani politics has been like the roulette. After every interregnum of civilian rule, the wheel starts all over again. The politicians mess up; the military takes over.

And as a dazed public looks down upon the sacked lot with anger and disgust and looks up to the incoming men in uniform with hopes and expectations the intellectual elite huddles into the quieter corners for its usual debate. Even the worst democracy is better than the most benign dictatorship, it proclaims.

For years, the intellectuals have been ardently arguing that an uninterrupted political process would in time throw up a more democratic, more representative and more effective leadership, more sensitive to the people's welfare than its own.

But the experience has been proving otherwise. After every turn, a still more rapacious civilian crowd walks in,

Indeed, the country's politics had a very pernicious start. Right at the outset, it came to be captured by a class that was bred, patronised and nurtured by the British colonialists to perpetuate their rule. The feudal lords and chieftains, generously rewarded with titles and privileges for their services to the Crown, and the bureaucrats, groomed to help rule the colony, took over the centre-stage of national politics. There was no outlet for the commoners to get into the power circle.

And as this greedy, avaricious and selfserving crowd scrambled for power, spoils and riches, they left the poor masses out in the cold. And while this clan of adventurists kept growing more powerful, richer and more corrupt, it gave to the poor masses flour mixed with sand to eat and tea mixed with chickpea peel to drink.

With its shenanigans, the clan took away the people's faith in civilian rule, transformed their hopes for a better future into bleak despair, and turned their sweet dream of a prosperous Pakistan sour.

The masses saw a ray of hope in Ayub Khan's basic democracies, promising to give them a leadership from the grass roots, fully alive to their problems, needs and demands. And the institution, despite all its flaws, did have the potential to spawn a new breed of political leaders with humble background that in time could have broken the monopoly of the privileged over national politics.

And to some extent, it did produce the results. Not only ordinary people were elected as basic democrats in great strength, they gave urgently needed brick streets, rural roads, primary schools, dispensaries, post offices and other small services to their electorates.

But the institution had only a short life. It died with the fall of Ayub Khan, without showing its full promise.

Anyway, Zulfikar Ali Bhutto got a chance to liberate the nation's politics from the domination of the privileged class and lay the foundations for a fully representative, responsive and public-minded leadership to emerge.

Not only had he won massive support from the downtrodden sections of society and the sizeable middle class that had come up in the wake of economic development in Ayub Khan's time. The electorate had also sent up members of ordinary background in quite a strength to the legislatures under the banner of his Pakistan People's Party in the 1970 poll.

But he frittered away this invaluable opportunity. His own lust for power and unchallenged authority proved too overpowering. Instead of promoting a pluralistic political order, he, like his mentor Ayub Khan, set out to eliminate all rival centres of power and stifle all voices of dissent.

Never shy of taking pride on being perhaps the world's only civilian martial law administrator, an anathema to a true democrat, he emasculated his political opponents with strong arm. And with his nationalisation gun, he shot down an emerging powerful middle class along with big industrialists and businessmen.

At through his first tenure, he allowed his opponents to hold a public rally only; once, at Rawalpindi, but unleashed on it the goons of his notorious federal security force who handed down several dead bodies to the organisers to carry home.

Though with favours, perks and money, he created a vast cadre of party workers, he pampered a section of the landed aristocracy to act as his local power-brokers. Promoting a grassroots leadership to back him up was not in his mind.

And when he called the 1977 poll, apart from that large crowd of his party stalwarts who, like him, got themselves elected unopposed with the help of state power, the candidates figuring up on his list for the contest mostly belonged to this aristocracy, not to the under-privileged classes.

The bouts of civilian rumpus, military rules and autocratic dispensations were thought to have driven home some lessons to the political lights. And as the new series of civilian rule started in 1985, it was believed that an era of a more sensible and more representative democratic dispensation would ensue.

But that was not to be. The rapacious lot was again back in business. As the middle class had further shrunk in the face of an exploding population, runaway poverty and stagnant economy, national politics stood polarised around the person of Zulfikar Ali Bhutto, and the political parties had largely lost touch with the masses the clan found the field wide open to it.

There was only one difference. The tribe was now not exclusively a landed aristocracy thing. It had now also quite an intake of industrialists and businessmen. Indeed, class distinctions had largely obliterated in the clan, as the feudal lords had also forked out into industries and business while the *industrialists and businessmen had ventured out into real estate and farming as well.*

The dominant stars of this new era were Benazir Bhutto and Nawaz Sharif. Both spoke of the poor. But under them, only the privileged flourished. And both polls and politics became the plaything of only the moneyed class.

Just give a look to the legislatures that came up at the centre and in the provinces from the past four polls. They had almost the same familiar faces, either sitting on one side of the aisle after one poll and on the other side after the next.

And a measure of their concern about the electorate's welfare could well be had from the issues they agitated on the floors of the house. As terrorists, for instance, were mowing down innocent worshippers outside, inside the house they were grossly preoccupied about the production of an incarcerated senator.

And while the destitute and the unemployed were committing suicides in droves outside, the honourable legislators inside were more concerned about the insolence of a PIA minion for not according due courtesies including class upgradation to one of their colleagues.

Indeed, only the most enthusiast would say that these past 15 years of democratic rule have given a leadership that really represents the man on the street and really cares for him.

The problem is that the issues that agitate our intellectual elite the most are the issues that agitate our common man the least. For it, democracy is an end in itself. For him, it isn't. For it, what matters the most are the freedoms of thought, expression and action. For him, it is the freedom from hunger, unemployment, poverty and disease.

What really matter to him are the issues of bread and butter. And those can best be tackled if he can send to the legislature and the government representatives who understand what are his real problems, what needs to be addressed urgently and what can be put off for the time being.

Unless fundamental electoral reforms are brought in to provide such a representation and liberate legislatures and governments from the stranglehold of the privileged and moneyed class, no amount of continuity in political activity can give a durable, lasting and workable democratic system. Real democracy would remain a dream; and the roulette would keep moving again and again.

---

* Courtesy : *The Frontier Post (Pakistan)*

7

A Close Run Thing

** Kamran Shafi*

Greetings to all those doubting Thomases (and Janes). Didn't I say so? Didn't I say that the frayed and tattered fabric of the country just couldn't take all that "The Family" was throwing at it? Didn't I say that there was nothing like "There will never be another army intervention; the days of coups d'etat are over; America won't stand for it" and other such inane rubbish? Of course, all the time I was saying what I was, my heart was in my mouth, I was hoping against hope that there would be someone who would come to the nation's rescue. Well, it was a close run thing. But, when its happened, and may Allah be praised.

One should have thought that there was no point at all in going over the right royal mess the two dolts from Gowalmandi made of the country. I, among others, having said enough about it. One should have thought that the time was here now to look to the future and to see where we should go from here. But one cannot ignore the cowardly and mean and downright criminal acts of "The Family", and their retainers in the closing hours of their iniquitous, greedy and wicked rule. One cannot ignore the shameful roles played by the arrogant Saeed Mehdi, said to be the richest bureaucrat in the whole world, which is saying something when there are such serious contenders for the slot as Salman

Farooqui and others; Khawaja Ziauddin who does not deserve to be called a general, Shahid Khaqan Abbassi and Aminullah Chaudhry and Rana Maqbool in trying to assassinate General Pervaiz Musharraf. Look at the limits to which these scum were willing to go to sow dissension in the army's ranks, and to finally throw the country into utter chaos just to save their liege's miserable skin.

Look at the extent to which "The Family" had criminalised the government itself when four of the highest officials of state were ready to do murder for their lord. By preventing the plane carrying General Musharraf from landing, they cared not a whit for the hundreds of other innocent passengers, including a party of schoolchildren on board the aircraft. Well, I, for one, have always considered "The Family" to be criminal and cruel to the core, but were all of these people so criminal, too? It boggles the senses to see "friends" of Nawaz Sharif, people like Major Ikram Sehgal, continue to call him a "nice man". Would a "nice man" have considered mass murder? Nice man? Help us, dear God. The prosecution should not allow any of the accused to turn approver. They should all fact trial, and if convicted, be locked up forever, the key to their cells thrown into one of the ornamental ponds on the Ittefaq estate.

Look at Ziauddin. Did 35 years of wearing the uniform of the Pakistan Army not instill any honour in him at all? Was he that brazen and faithless that he willingly joined the coup against his own chief? Was he that foolish that in spite of heading the much-vaunted Inter-Services Intelligence (ISI) he did not know the mood of the army? Was he that taken in by the love and affection showered upon Shahbaz Sharif and himself, as emissaries of a "favourite" government, at the mecca of all our politicians, Washington, DC? It is obvious, is it not that fools surround themselves with fools? But there were other players, too.

Look at the role the United States has played in this drama. It is obvious, is it not that Washington had a big part to play (foolishly, and shamefully, yet again) in the attempted destabilisation of the army? There are reports in the press of the

Americans being aware of plans to sack General Musharraf, which were discussed during Ziauddin's pilgrimage. Instead of cautioning reason and trying to instill some little good sense into their satraps, the Sharif Brothers Inc, the Americans seem to have sanctioned their every move. How obscene. Was President Clinton to Nawaz Sharif what Valery Giscard D'estaing, the former French president, was to Emperor Bokassa of the Central African Empire?

I have long been an ardent admirer of President Clinton, and have often argued that he is, by far, the most brilliant of US presidents of recent memory; that he is the most well-informed of them; the most well-spoken and quickest on his feet; the most caring. I thought that a president who has the time to visit the smallest school and discuss the growing violence in schools with the children, and to try and devise solutions, on the very day that he was being impeached could not but be a good man. But, see how his administration molly-coddled Mr. Sharif who was no less than a dictator, and a very empty-headed one at that. I am appalled.

Look at Mushahid Hussain, whose motto became "karrake kad dian gey, Oye", just as soon as he entered Mr. Sharif's service. While people blamed Mushahid for most of Sharif's idocies, and have long held that he would be responsible for Mr. Sharif's final departure from politics, I did not quite agree with them because I have always had great faith in Mr. Sharif's own innate foolishness and wickedness. But see what he does. Mushahid, who always portrayed himself as the army's man, is accused too of a part in hatching the diabolical plan during Mr. Sharif's ill-omened junket to Abu Dhabi. God, the fiendishness of it all!

But, to the future. Having pulled us out of the raging river of deceit and ignominy into which the Sharifs had plunged the hapless people of this country, General Musharraf now stands at a crossroads, the nation, shivering with cold and fear lined up behind him. Two of the roads lead to ambushes laid by politicians of varying hues, clamouring to give him false counsel and to then inveigle their way into power. Both of these roads lead to sure disaster. There is only one road to take. The general must go it alone; he must remain aloof and distant; he must keep politicians at arm's length, let alone ask them for counsel. He must particularly stay away from the pretender political parties such a Imran Khan's Tehreek-e-Insaf, and more specially Sardar Farooq's Millat Party, the leaders of which ran the worst, and most intellectually dishonest government it has been the misfortune of this country to have ever had. There are enough good people, not tainted by self-service politics, who can help him. More than anything else the general must wield a big stick in the form of his right boot, and use it often and hard, without fear or favour, without rancour or hate.

There is so much to do; look around you, at anything, and you will see it needs fixing. The chief executive must identify a few areas that can be fixed in short order, such as swift accountability across the board. Everyone knows everyone else's worth before they were thrust into power—with those convicted being jailed for long terms and debarred from politics for life. Which reminds me: what is Ijazul Haq doing going about with a halo around his head asking for other people's accountability? How about his own? The regime must purge the police of the goondas inducted by successive governments. It must smash the qubza groups which operate in every tehsil and district headquarters, the local MNAs and MPAs, the police and the district revenue departments their partners in crime; widows and orphans, the weak and the gentle, their victims.

It's a tall order, but then General Musharraf has proved himself to be a soldier's soldier. I must caution him however: the Sharifs were in power for too long. Their tentacles are spread throughout the land specially in their fief, the Punjab. Purge all their agents first-off, and watch your back. They are criminals such as the world has never seen before, and hopefully will never see again.

I must remark in passing that Ms. Benazir Bhutto's interview on BBC World left me gasping with disbelief. To term the coup a "civil war" was silly in the extreme. It almost sounded like wishful thinking and caused much consternation in the country.

One is gratified that there has been a massive shake-up in our embassies abroad—it must now engulf those who sit in the Hotel Shehrezade too, and who acquiesced to Mr Sharif's every whim, every silliness. The disgraceful heroin smuggling affair of June 1997 and which humiliated this country must be thoroughly and vigorously investigated. The unfair sacking of officers, in one case ordered by Mr. Sharif's now disgraced military secretary, must be redressed.

More strength to your boot, general, and may God keep you in His care.

---

* Courtesy : *The Pakistan Times,* October, 21,1999

8

Nation Tormented at Democrats' Hands

* *Air Marshal (Retd.) Ayaz Ahmad Khan*

Four elected governments have fallen in disgrace during the last ten years. They all earned disrepute and notoriety, and each one of them caused immense damage to Pakistan's economy and polity. All the four government, two under Benazir Bhutto and two under Mian Nawaz Sharif have one thing in common—they subotaged people's mandate and subverted democracy for self-aggrandisement and perpetuation of power.

The first PPP government under Benazir Bhutto fell in disgrace after only 20 months in office, ie. October 1988 to August 1990. Benazir Bhutto had disfigured democracy by corruption, nepotism and mismanagement. Nawaz Sharif's first ML government lasted two and a half years in Nov. 1990 to Feb. 1993. He was sacked by GIK for nepotism, corruption, and financial bungling, but was restored into office by the Supreme Court.

Both the PML and the president were sent home by General Waheed Kakar. The feud between the president and the prime minister and their dismissal by the army chief was a setback for democracy. PPP's second government under Benazir Bhutto was dismissed after three years by President Sardar Farooq Ahmed Khan Leghari for making a mess of administration and institutions, and for gross interference by Asif Ali Zardari, prime minister's spouse, in the affairs of the state. BB violated all the norms of democracy and paid the price for it.

The second Muslim League regime under Nawaz Sharif got into hot water due to mismanagement of economy soon after the May 28-31 Chagai nuclear tests. His dictatorial style had stifled democracy, and made all institutions of the state dysfunctional. His insane plot to dismiss and kidnap General Pervaiz Musharraf, chairman Joint Chief of Staff Committee and Chief of the Army Staff backfired. Nawaz Sharif derailed democracy. Democracy has been chief victim of the misrule by PPP and Muslim League governments. They are responsible for harming Pakistan and denying the masses the fruits of freedom, democracy, economic security and social progress.

Benazir stormed into power with public support in October 1988. Twenty months later she was out of office. During the first PPP regime all state organisations and departments were filled with 'jahil jayalas'. These included WAPDA, PIA, banks and DFIs. Top and middle-level bureaucracy was dealt with a vengeance. The so-called loyalists and political fundos replaced professionals. The PPP government disregarded merit and professionalism. Shifarish, and chits and telephone calls from PPP influentials were required for every thing. This paralysed administration and institutions. Parliament and assemblies were marginalised and MNAs and MPAs became rubber stamps. Pushed by Zardari Benazir targeted Pakistan's banking system, and financial institutions into submission. Nationalised banks were ordered to give large loans to relatives and favoured pals.

Zardari and his cronies obtained loans amounting to Rs. 660 crore i.e. Rs. 6,600 million for the establishing sugar mills. Three times this amount was loaned to favourites for cement plants. Corporate scam, Taj Company collapse and collapse of the banking system took place during BB's first tenure in office. Law and order was in shambles and criminals and dacoits ruled the roost in Sindh. BB brought peace to Karachi by settling scores with the MQM by eliminating over 2000 MQM armed activists. But in rest of the country murders and crime continued unabated. Sectarian killers targeted 'Masajid' and 'namazis' were butchered during prayer time. Law and order remained out of control. BB was insincere on Kashmir, even Kashmir House board was removed to please Rajiv Gandhi. She was soft on India especially on the Kashmir issue.

The tormented nation was spared from further torture and agony when GIK on the advice of Aslam Beg, sacked Benazir's shockingly corrupt regime in August 1990. Her unceremonious exit weakened democracy.

During Nawaz Sharif's first tenure the corporate scam exploded and billions of savings of the poor and of the middle class were washed away. Taj Company went under and the victims were not treated fairly. GIK objected to Nawaz Sharif's despotic style and the orders from PM house to the nationalised banks to dole out billions to cronies, relations and friends in total disregard of banking rules and regulations. Institutions remained paralysed as before, and while the banks were emptied, personal coffers of the influentials and mega-barons started overflowing. Mega projects like the Motorway, yellow cab, tractor, and boat schemes were started which caused huge losses to the banking sector. GIK's advice that nationalised banks should be allowed to invest for profit, and not for the political gains and benefit of the rulers was disregarded. Nawaz Sharif showed defiance and confronted the president needlessly and wrongly. His undemocratic posture and whimsical policies harmed democracy. GIK dismissed Nawaz Sharif for pilferage and plunder. The army was watching the mockery of democracy from high perch and pounced to clear the decks. Prime Minister Nawaz Sharif and President Ghulam Ishaq were both sacked by then COAS General Wahid Kakar on April 11, 1993. But the political rulers learnt no lession.

Benazir bounced back into power for the second time in August 1995 and resorted to loot and plunder. She started stifling democracy from the outset Asif Zardari ruled the roost and acted virtually as prime minister of Pakistan. He was made minister of investment with out the ministry of investment.

The husband and wife started the culture of loot-khasoot in right earnest. By obtaining billion of rupees loans from nationalised banks under fictitious names, and ripping of state deals by hefty commissions. Asif Ali Zardari became a moneyed tycoon overnight. He shovelled billions into foreign accounts with overseas banks in Dubai, Switzerland and British off-shore islands. This emanated a wave of anger and frustration all across Pakistan. But Benzir Bhutto remained totally oblivious to what her spouse was up to. The forex reserves had hit an all time low. FCA deposits were stolen so cleverly that they were found missing only after the exit of the second PPP regime.

Both Benazir and Asif Ali Zardari crudely disregarded norms of democratic governance. PPP MNAs shared the loot and greatly benefitted from the so-called development funds. Each PPP MNA got in excess of Rs. one crore and each PPP MPA Rs. fifty lakh. Not more than ten percent was spent on the people. With them the PPP jayalas also benefitted and the country became poor and the have-nots poorer as crooks plundered state coffers at will. Banks, WAPDA, PIA and several other state institutions and private organisations were directed by Asif Ali Zardari to contribute to improve ecology and environment. At a meeting Zardari disclosed that the nationalised banks had contributed Rs. 270 crore to his tree-plantation fund. No none knows where that money went.

---

* Courtesy : *The Frontier Post (Pakistan),* October, 30, 1999

9

Will We Be Deceived Twice?

** Anees Jillani*

I have yet to meet anyone in the Islamic Republic during the past one week who is opposed to the military takeover by General Pervaiz Musharraf. I am not surprised because I did not meet anyone during the past one year who had anything nice to say about the pervious government. What an irony because just a couple of years ago in February 1997, the people of Pakistan, including myself, had so overwhelmingly supported Nawaz Sharif and brought him to power. What brought about the downfall of Mr. Sharif in such a short span of time?

General Zia ul Haq ruled Pakistan with an iron hand from 1977 through 1985 and then through a civilian setup from 1985 until his death in August 1988. Despite his draconian measures, he could not finish the Bhutto family legacy and Benazir came to power through the first elections that she contested in her lifetime in 1988. By August 1990, the people were begging President Ghulam Ishaq Khan to get rid of her regime. What mistakes had Benazir made during her 1988-90 tenure and then during her 1993-1996 administration?

Both governments lacked vision and sincerity. They genuinely thought that the people of Pakistan are idiots and the richer and more powerful you get, the more the common man prostrates in front of you. During the 1985-1999 period when the civilians have been in power, what have they done for Pakistan? Ask Benazir this question and all she can think of right away is polio national immunisation days. She perhaps does not know that these immunisation days are being organised nowadays all over the world not by the governments but by Unicef through national governments; they are even funded by the international agency. Ask Mr. Sharif and he would mention the motorway. What a record?

Some would say that what have the military rulers like Ayub Khan, Yahya Khan and General Zia ul Haq done during their hold on power. The answer is simple. We did not elect them and we thus had no expectations from them. A wise man once said that experience is a comb which nature gives to men when they are bald.

I hope that the nation of Pakistan is not totally bald and still has some hair left despite repeated chemotherapy sessions. Many are getting impatient at the slow pace the present regime is moving. It is important to take one wise and strong step in the right direction rather than taking a hundered haphazard steps in all directions leading to Kargil, Afghanistan turmoil, sanctions following nuclear tests, devaluations, sales taxes, constant increase in gasoline prices and then retracting those steps.

I don't need to read Gallup Poll surveys to know that people want an across the board accountability of everyone who matters in this country. God has given General Musharraf this golden opportunity to serve the country and prove his mettle. He will not have this chance for ever. And he should not just concentrate on Mr. Sharif and his cohorts. People want the military to conduct a quick surgical operation of everyone in order not just to expose their misdeeds (we all know about them) but to punish them and then more importantly to recover the public money from them. Concentrating on just a fraction of the political spectrum would result in the same kind of witch-hunting that General Zia ul Haq indulged in for eleven long years.

And this process of accountability and reforms cannot be conducted by the lot that has been in power in this country for the past 52 years. This lot wearing crisp shalwar kameez twice a day with the latest mobile in one hand and a fancy key chain of Pajero or Honda VTI in the other hand is incapable of this kind of operation. They don't even want to do it and the question of their capacity consequently does not arise. They just wag their tails whoever comes to power. This lot could be seen hanging from Benazir's Pajero in the late '80s and then it was knocking at Mr. Sharif's doors a couple of years later. Now they are looking for contacts with GHQ. They think they are so wise!

The other extreme consists of fossils that consist of retired generals, retired senior civil servants and others who spent their tenures in office doing everything other than what they were expected to do for ameliorating the lot of this unfortunate country, but now suddenly have discovered a plethora of ideas to remedy the country's ills. All of them should instead concentrate in writing their memoirs and even articles but should be asked to give up their perk ambitions. Their experience may count in some cases and they should share it with the next generation; otherwise, who would play with the grandchildren?

Then we have a third category of wise men who left the country for greener pastures and ended up spending their golden years working for the World Bank, the IMF and multinationals. Now when they are approaching the end of their tenure in this world, they head home as if this is ghau shala (home for old cows) where they can die in peace and, if permitted by chance, why not enjoy the grade-22 perks.

If General Musharraf ends up collecting the above lot around him, then we, along with the general, are doomed. I use the strong word doomed because the country now is in a precarious position and cannot afford to undergo another status quo-oriented approach. I really don't mind it the government moves slow; however, whenever it acts, is should be a swift and clear-headed action without any second thoughts. Clean and honest folks should be brought on the government plank instead of the above lot because no miracles can be expected from the latter.

I will give the government only one example to prove my point. The takeover is less than a week old but the bank defaulters are already panicky. One bank acted smart and sent a letter to all its defaulters followed by personalised calls falsely informing them that they have been asked to forward a defaulters list to GHQ. If they wish their name not to be on the list, they should immediately make arrangements to clear their dues. It may sound unbelievable but more than 90 per cent responded with electrifying speed to inform the bank that they would try to clear their dues in the next two to three days and their names should not be placed on the list.

This scare will not last forever, in fact, it is likely to wither away in weeks and not months. It is now for the government to use this momentum and the present mass support and public goodwill to its advantage and move in the right direction. We all, of course, can wish General Musharraf our best wishes and support but remember if a man deceives us once, shame on him. However, if he deceives us twice, shame on us.

---

* Courtesy : *The Pakistan Times,* October, 25,1999

10

Necessity Makes Prohibited Things Permissible!

* *Ahmad Ali*

The proclamation of emergency and assuming complete administrative control of the country by the chief executive of Pakistan (CEOP) has brought Pakistan once again to the cross-roads. The questions as to whether this extra-constitutional step of the CEOP is justified, legally maintainable and what necessitated this grave step needs to be answered by reference to the obtainable conditions in the country. A few words, however, are necessary about the current legal arrangement.

The action of October 12, by keeping the Constitution of Pakistan (The Constitution) in abeyance and notifying the Provisional Constitution Order 1, of 1999, (PCO) has given rise to some interesting legal and academic discussion. It is being said, for example, that the judges of the superior courts are required to take a fresh oath under the PCO (the new legal order) as the Constitution (the old legal order) is no more in existence, at least for the time being. The other view is that there is no need to have a fresh oath as the Constitution has not been abrogated but merely kept in abeyance. For an academic discussion, the action (or re-action) of October 12, together with the PCO, obligates its careful examination.

The new legal order consists of two parts i.e. the Proclamation of Emergency and the PCO. The proclamation is issued by the Chairman Joint Chiefs of Staffs Committee (CJCSC) who is also the Chief of Army Staff (COAS). Through this proclamation the Constitution is kept in abeyance. The CJCSC/ COAS has assumed to himself the powers of the CEOP and has ordered the suspension of the National and Provincial Assemblies and the Senate. The prime minister, all chief ministers, federal ministers, advisors, provincial as well as federal have been sacked.

The second step being taken is the issuance of the PCO which prescribes the new legal order. Article 2 (1) of the PCO maintains that notwithstanding the abeyance of the provisions of the Constitution the country shall be governed, subject to PCO, as nearly as possible in accordance with the (held-up) Constitution. Sub-clause (2) of Article 2 allows the conditional functioning of the courts in that they will not have the powers to make any order against the CE or any person exercising powers under his authority. Article 2 sub-clause (3) specifically allows the enforcement of fundamental rights as long as their enforcement is not in conflict with the new legal order. Article 7 enjoins that all persons in the service of Pakistan and those who immediately before such commencement were in office as judge of the SC, the FSC or a High Court or Auditor-General or Ombudsman and Chief Ehtesab Commissioner, shall continue in the said service on the same terms and conditions and shall enjoy the same privileges, if any. Finally the PCO declares that the whole of Pakistan will come under the control of the armed forces of Pakistan.

The proclamation of emergency and the enforcement of New Legal Order is not something unknown in this country and the courts are dealing with this issue since 1958 when General Ayub proclaimed full-fledged martial law for the first time in the history of Pakistan. Earlier in 1954 an impasse or legal breakdown resulted after the decision by the Federal Court in Maulvi Tamizuddin Khan's case (PLD 1955 FC 240). In that case the Federal Court had held that all laws passed by the Constituent Assembly required the governor-general's assent. This led to a constitutional and administrative breakdown as the governor-general had not assented to around 44 acts passed by the Constituent Assembly under which hundreds of orders had been issued and judicial decisions were taken. In addition, the acts done, actions taken and legislation made by the provincial legislatures also became invalid. The governor-general later tried to validate those laws through the Emergency Powers Ordinance, 1955, which was declared as of no legal effect by the Federal Court in the Usif Patel Case (PLD 1955 FC 387). To wriggle out of this deadlock, a reference was filed by the governor-general to the Federal Court (PLD 1955 FC 435) asking it as to what would be an appropriate course to get out of this statement? The Federal Court while expressing its opinion, inter alia, validated all such laws under the common law of civil or state necessity. Thus for the first time in the constitutional history of Pakistani or perhaps in South Asia, the principle of state necessity was applied to avert a serious constitutional and administrative crisis.

In 1958 when General Ayub Khan declared martial law, the Supreme Court of Pakistan in a constitutional criminal appeal, applying the doctrine of Legal Positivism proposed by Hands Kelsen held that "where a constitution and the National Legal Order under it is disrupted by an abrupt political change not within the contemplation of the constitution, then such a change is called a revolution". It observed that "any change, no matter how and by whom brought about, whether by violence or non-violent coup d'etat or even by a person already in a public position, is in law a revolution if it annual the constitution and the annulment is effective". It viewed that "a victorious revolution or a successful coup d'etat is an internationally recognised legal method of changing a constitution and that after a change of the character has taken place, the national legal order must for its validity depend upon the new law-creating organ. Even courts lose their existing jurisdictions, and can function only to the extent and in the manner determined by the new Constitution". (State V. Dosso. PLD 1958 SC 533). The court argued that if a revolution or a coup d'eat satisfies the test of 'efficacy', it becomes a basic law-creating fact. Thus complete reliance was placed by the court on what it perceived was the Kelsen's Pure Theory of Law.

The Supreme Court of Pakistan in the Asma Jilani Case (PLD 1972 SC 139) maintained that the doctrine of legal positivism as propounded by Kelsen was mis-interpreted and incorrectly applied in the Dosso case. It declared the martial law of General Yahya as illegal but had to take recourse to the doctrine of necessity to save the country from a disaster.

Similarly in the Nusrat Bhutto Case (PLD 1977 SC 657) the Supreme Court upheld the principle of state necessity as enunciated in the Reference by HE the governor-general discussed above. The court rejected the Kelsen's Pure Theory of Law as a universally accepted theory and declined its strict application on the ground that the military takeover (of 1977) was not a revolution in Kelsenian terms. The court observed that "although the Armed Forces are undoubtedly in effective control of the administration, it is neither their intention nor indeed have they established a new legal order in suppression of the exiting legal order". It justified and legitimised the martial law proclaimed on July 5, 1977, as a constitutional deviation rather than the destruction of the old legal order.

A careful examination of the rule laid down in the Nusrat Bhutto case reveals that exceeding stress was placed on the conditions obtaining in the country which necessitated the imposition of martial law and was given due consideration in justifying the action of the CMLA by calling it a 'constitutional deviation'. The question as to whether it was a revolution or not, diminished in the background.

It follows that the courts in Pakistan have in variably followed the principle "I quod alias non est licitum, necessitas licitum facit" (that which otherwise is not lawful, necessity makes lawful). The courts have also upheld the principle that "the safety of the people and safety of the state is the supreme law". The only two incidents where the principle of necessity was ignored by the courts were firstly, in the Maulvi Tamizuddin Khan Case (PLD 1955 FC

240) and secondly, in the Mian Mohammed Nawaz Sharif Case (PLD 1993 SC…).

In the first case, the decision of the Federal Court that any legislation passed by the constituent assembly will not be a law, unless assented to by the governor-general, created a grave situation, discussed earlier. Conceiving the grave consequences, the Federal Court in response to the reference filed by HE the governor-general provided interim and conditional relief to the government. Strictly speaking, the court in the Maulvi Tamizuddin case also tried to avert a crisis by choosing, in its opinion, the lesser evil, that is, it maintained the status quo by reversing the decision of the Chief Court of Sindh on a technical ground.

The Chief Court of Sindh had earlier declared the dissolution of the Constituent Assembly by the governor-general as unconstitutional. However, in the process the Federal Court invalidated a large number of laws and constitutional acts which it validated subsequently.

In the latter case, the deposed prime minister whose government was dismissed by the president, after his restoration by the Supreme Court, resigned and dissolved the National Assembly despite the fact that the court had intervened and provided relief to the ousted PM by restoring his government.

These two instances suggest that once there is a breakdown, administrative or constitutional, no matter what damage-control measures are adopted, a tangible way out is absolutely necessary to avoid a total disaster. In addition, the courts have favoured a mechanism in the Constitution by which such type of constitutional failures could be forestalled. An effort was made in 1985 to provide such a mechanism by adding sub-Article (b) to Article 58(2) which empowered a president to dissolve the National Assembly in his own discretion. This device was described as a 'safety valve' but it lost its utility due to its excessive use by different presidents.

The question as to whether the judges of the superior courts are required to take a fresh oath under the PCO appears to be of no significance. There can be arguments for and against it. For example, by administering oaths to the newly appointed governors the chief justices of various high courts have 'impliedly' accepted and recognised the new legal order. Secondly, the courts are still functioning and conducting their day-to-day business notwithstanding the Constitution being held in abeyance. The other view is that in past judges were administered fresh oath under the new legal order, specially when the question was one of keeping the Constitution in abeyance as compared to its abrogation. Therefore according to this view point, it is necessary that the members of the superior judiciary must take a fresh oath under the new legal order, no matter how brief this pause is going to be.

Notwithstanding this trivial debate, the actual issue is to determine the status of the new legal order. The classic jurists, specially the realists like Austin, look on law as the command of the sovereign. This sovereign is not the parliament but the judges, for the realists, the sovereign is the court. If previous decisions of the courts can be of any guidance, in the absence of the old legal order, the action of October 12 can exclusively be judged on the touch-stone of the objective conditions and the effectiveness of the new legal order, its acceptance by the people and acquieseence by the state machinery. The response of the international community, international media, the support of the Commonwealth delegation to Pakistan and local enthusiasm suggests that the new administration has passed the test of 'efficacy'.

In order to overcome the constitutional crisis, it appears, there are two options, as suggested by the late Justice Munir in Governor-General's Reference: to cross the gap with a legal bridge or to hurtle into the chasm beyond any hope to rescue. The new administration may approach the Supreme Court to get a legal cover on the touch-stone of the doctrine of 'legal realism' and the principles laid down in the Reference by HE the governor-general (1955) and the Nusrat Bhutto Case (1977). In the alternative it may approach the political sovereign, the people of Pakistan, for a vote on its action of October 12 through a constitutional device i.e. the referendum. It will provide the CEOP a high moral ground to initiate his seven point agenda and to take appropriate constitutional, legal and administrative steps to provide good governance to the country. Now that an extereme step has been taken, it is in the interest of the country that it must be carried to its logical conclusion. It is the responsibility of the new administration to fulfil what it has promised or undertaken—to provide a clean and transparent government.

---

* Courtesy : *The Pakistan Times,* October, 25,1999

11

No Coup D'etat, But Coup de Grace

* *Rehmat Shah Afridi*

The latest change in Pakistan should not be labelled as coup d'etat. It is good riddance; riddance of a government utterly devoid of all norms of social, ethical and democratic behaviour. In fact, the rulers had themselves sown the seeds of the coup. The Pakistan Army only dealt a coup de grace to the despotic rule unleashed on the humanity reeling under multi-faceted crises. Has Mian Nawaz Sharif and his cronies ever taken any interest in national or democratic development? Should not we ask where the constitutional stalwarts, who are issuing statements today, were rusting when the Nawaz-led government, mandated to safeguard the Constitution, had made criminal advances on the most sanctimonious of the institutions in the country? The then rulers had virtually rebelled against the Constitution by attacking the Supreme Court. They meted out beastly treatment to the superior judiciary. In a sense, they were justified in razing to the ground the facade of the most essential pillars of the state, because they had no moral courage to refrain from interfering in sub judice matters. They trespassed all ethical bounds. One would never expect such a ghastly act from the beasts in the jungle. Today, these daredevil violators of the law of the land hatched a conspiracy to arrest the chief of army staff of Pakistan. They are capable of going to any extent to uphold their despotic rule. I wonder if they would not mete out the unrelenting treatment to the honourable judges of the Supreme Court to stay in the power corridors. Was the appointment of Ghous Ali Shah as advisor on the turbulent affairs of the Sindh province legal when the public representatives were functioning and the democratic institutions were still intact? Had the constitutional stalwarts taken any practical step for the rights of Sindh in other provinces? Is democracy the name of a one-family rule? Is putting up with a corrupt ruler democracy? Were extra-judicial killings not taking place in Sindh and Punjab? Had Mian Nawaz Sharif not compelled in the dialect of civil martial law the members of the Parliament to keep silent? Was not Nawaz Sharif throwing the Constitution into a blind well in the future? Had Nawaz not wrested the national banks and government land of billions of dollars illegally? Has the ousted prime minister not made billions from his illegal business? I wonder if it is not disrespect to the Constitution in general and the humanity in particular that saving the country from disintegration was callously labelled as "rebellion".

If the then prime minister had succeeded in getting arrested the chief of the army staff by an inspector of police, would the heads of the remaining institutions not have accepted the personal servitude of Nawaz? Where was the Constitution paid any respect? Were the illegal and unconstitutional courts in Sindh for the sake of the people? Or were the courts meant to indemnify the Nawaz government? Was that not an insult to the Constitution? Was it correct on the part of the government to allocate crores of rupees to the members of the NWFP Assembly after parting ways with the Awami National Party to stay basking in the sun of governmental powers? The way Mian Nawaz insulted the Constitution cannot be expected from a dictator. Had Nawaz Sharif delegated any authority to the Election Commission or the election commissioner? The worth of assets Mian Nawaz Sharif had declared before the Election Commission was less than the worth of his watch. His personal assets abroad come to billions of dollars. The legal brains of the country witnessed the driving of the last nail in the coffin of Constitution whereof they talk so boastfully.

The Constitution lies buried for the last so many years. Which Constitution you are talking of? The one which Nawaz insulted as a democratic right not only in his court, but also in his toilet. I would like to ask my friends who are less tired of talking about the Constitution these days if they had not said a number of times that Mian Nawaz Sharif murdered both the federation and the Constitution. Their statements are still on the record of the newspapers. Therefore, they are advised to talk of drafting a fresh and transparent constitution. They have themselves uttered time and again that it was long enough that the present Constitution was distorted, then why we are shedding crocodile tears.

We should be down to earth. A strict and across-the-board-accountability should be conducted in all earnestness. If we did no make the right decision at the moment, I believe a terrible rebellion would take place on the streets and then there would be no one even to talk of the Constitution.

I should like to quote an adage: If your luck slumbers, you must not quit your waking. I call upon the present dispensation to conduct only transparent accountability of yourselves and others, only then we can hope that the country would be known as a true democratic and constitutional state in the outer world. If my worthy friends doubt the veracity of my claim, they should consult history. Once our Prophet Mohammed (Peace Be Upon Him) was asked as to who was the most mischievous person, the Prophet replied that the scholar who had gone astray. So, I would like to advise my friends that if we would take pride in our wisdom, we may become mischievous. You must know better than me as you command more knowledge that when a man gives way to animal instincts, he becomes more dangerous than the animal itself.

Today, our friendly countries are very much concerned about our well-being that democracy has come to an end in Pakistan. Perhaps those who are not even acquainted with this country know better about democracy in Pakistan than I do.

As far as I know about democracy, it hardly comprises the things which our dear Mian Nawaz Sharif has introduced to it. I wonder if the worthy readers are oblivious of the number of gang ropes committed every day. Have we ever raised voice for their rights? You know that Mian Nawaz had set a dual criterion for the victims of gang-rapes. He would publicise the unfortunate victims of the smaller provinces on the electronic media and would heap more humiliation on the poor families. Regarding the victims in the Punjab province, newspapers offices would be directed to downplay such incidents as it would foment law and order situation, whereas the victims of criminal assaults in Sindh would be advertised on the television time and again. Was it a feast of democracy? Is there any one who does not know about the fact that the personal force of Nawaz, the elite force, comprised a cross section of the society, having among its ranks all sorts of criminals, businessmen, government employees and legal brains? We all knew it very well, but we were silent because of democracy.

The elderly people used to say that a proud man can make friends with no body, because friendship need equality among friends. This saying well suits Mian Nawaz. I think the ousted prime minister badly lacked this quality. No one can advise a proud and haughty man; it demands superiority, which Nawaz Sharif holds in bitter despise.

Those people who join the government of Nawaz Sharif used to be very much clean and true, but when they utilise their democratic right, they are labeled as traitors and terrorists. And whenever they again join the camp of Nawaz Sharif, they are all cleansed of the stinking blemish. Is it not tantamount to the trampling of democracy and revolt against the Constitution? You must be all knowing that the party of Mian Nawaz Sharif had obtained only 10 lakh votes is Sindh. The two majority parties, PPP and MQM, were not given the right to form the government in the Sindh province. This also speaks volumes for the love Mian Nawaz Sharif has for democracy.

Does Ghous Ali Shah, who himself is well versed in the law of the land, not usurp the public rights when he became the chief advisor to the prime minister on Sindh affairs? Can the modus operandi which Nawaz Sharif employed for removing the

Chief of Army Staff, General Pervaiz Musharraf, be employed by any person who claims to love democracy and the Constitution? Can Mr. Nawaz be trusted in any way? Whenever he entered a promise, it was but for his selfish needs and personal benefit. He talked of ridding the country of the scourge of interest based economy; but first he would claim billions on account of interest for himself and then would claim the interest for the country.

You must have come across the news item that Nawaz Sharif has sold out the Lahore Camp Jail on a thrown away price to a Korean company and that Mian Shahbaz Sharif has received Rs. 40 million as commission in advance. When our brave soldiers were shedding their blood for the integrity of the country on the Kargil front, India had launched a fund raising campaign for their armed forces. The same Korean company, which has almost purchased the worth Rs. 2 billion land of the Camp Jail without having floated any tender, donated the lion's share to the Indian army. This is also a token of love Nawaz Sharif has for democracy. And is making more than Rs. 20 billion in less than 10 years also a part of democracy? And making the press council was also the obsessive love of the then prime minister and his worthy information minister, Mushahid Hussain, for the freedom of expression in the country. Was the propaganda which Mr. Mushahid had unleashed to malign the Pakistan Army through some paid elements a token of his love for democracy and the country?

Elders say if you do not want to help your friend in distress, then you should not ask him about his grievances, because this is hypocrisy.

On the one hand, Mian Nawaz Sharif was making billions from selling sugar to India at a time when our brave soldiers were engaged in sacrificing their lives in Kashmir for the sake of the country. The sugar would be sold out to India only to be re-imported from Dubai. How much the rulers were in love with democracy! On the other hand, the prime minister earned at least Rs. 3 billion in the spare parts of vehicles by issuing SROs from the Ministry of Commerce. This was the types of love they had for the people and the country and this was necessary for the survival of democracy.

Bacon has said that the conspiracy hatched for satisfying hunger is the worst. If we do not have any regard for commanding respect after a good half a century, our friends would hardly respect us. The other nations of the world would never stand by us at the time of our trial.

We should not forget the dismemberment of Pakistan in 1971. The integrity of the country is necessary; constitutions would keep on making and unmaking, but making a country falls to the lot of honest and true people. We know our lot very well. We should pray for the integrity of the country.

There are scores of honest people and men of character in the motherland, but they are silent for their honour. Herbert Spencer says that the loosening of character, not the lack of knowledge, often leads to weakening of the decision-making power. Pakistan is the only land of the world where the people are homeless despite having a home; where the people have been plundered several times, but they do not raise any voice for their rights; where the looters and plunderers in democratic robes are never tired of calling their people illiterate. A lettered goof can easily conceal his ignorance under euphemism, but it would still be stupidity (Franklin). If we are industrious, we would never come to face famine, for famine can hardly knock at the doors of hard-working people; it only glances at their courtyards from outside. The only good question on the earth is that what I can do for averting the ugly situation (Franklin).

Therefore, I would like to tell my friends that we have to make the decision to break the begging bowel, unlike Nawaz Sharif who can stoop to be a royal beggar and still reminds his people that they have made the atomic bomb; who asks the people to eat grass, but himself commits worth crores of rupees of dacoity daily. No, we will have to forsake hypocrisy for dealing with an honest people, lest we should literally face a coup.

---

* Courtesy : *The Frontier Post (Pakistan)*, October 11, 1999

12

No Tears for Democracy?

* *Rifaat Hamid Ghani*

Covering General Pervaiz Musharraf's takeover of the government on October 12, the international media reflected a western bafflement bordering on exasperation with Pakistan's complaisance at the exchange of a self-inducted general for a democratically-anointed prime minister. After all, the suddenly incarcerated prime minister had won the 1997 elections by a majority so heavy as to have empowered him to change the constitution quite legally.

And that became the root and essence of the political problem, for the people mistrusted the direction of change that had become uncontrollable as checks and balances were dismantled or neutralised one by one. They feared the concentration of power and they questioned the judgement of the individual in whom it was invested. They were delighted to see him go and that immediate problem solved.

But why did it have to happen that way, and what have they got now? They are certainly in no more effective control of the government they receive or will receive. Whereas before they could claim a right to speak up, that right is now on sufferance.

Why it had to happen that way is not just because the parliamentary opposition was weak or the street-power of political opposition not demonstrable enough or because the people rejected the political alternatives available. It also had to happen that way because Gen. Musharraf was on board a commercial flight with 200 other passengers, and was disinclined to have it crash-land through lack of fuel. Gen. Musharraf had to act then or not at all.

People were more than able to sympathise if he did not want to be whisked off and away from a strip at Nawabshah or left holding the buck for landing in India. Pakistanis were horrified at the prime minister's cavalier approach to disinvesting a chief of army staff and chairman Joint Chiefs of Staff Committee of office. Procedural formalities having been dispensed with as it were, the people were on the side of the general. The sense of national self-preservation told them it was essential to keep the army intact as a unified professional institution.

But did preserving military unity and obedience to the high command have to become a confirmed suspension of the ongoing political process? And is that what people want given the level of democratic malfunction and political venality? The induction of military power is viewed in relation to a civilian political opposition that is too weak to achieve its own ends. This very considerable though ineffectual opposition to Mr. Sharif encompassed political parties inside and outside of parliament and their adherents; as well as a vast unaligned mass that was as disillusioned with those parties as it was rejectionist of Mr. Sharif's government and partymen. It is this mass that demagogues can sway; whose discontent oligarchs and Bonapartists can exploit; and which exponents of a third democratic force that needs time and opportunity to emerge and develop, with caretaker regimes that promise that back-cloth, can address.

It now seems that the general in effecting what he prefers to call a counter-coup is putting his weight behind the development of a third force. A cocktail of caretakers under the dignifying rubric of a National Security Council, in the absence of martial law and an abeyance of constitutional structure, will manage things as the COAS and chief executive deems best. Like almost all Pakistanis at the moment he is rejecting the practitioners of democracy but not democracy itself. Is this sustainable?

There is a fundamental distinction not just between the civil and the military mind but between civil and military social organisation. In terms of the individual, the one accommodates the gamut of human social needs the other does not: The most dedicated of soldiers needs his mufti and come out of uniform.

But when the military mind and method is in command and control of the civil political process it cannot take turns with democratic relaxation for civvies. Instead of a civilised society we have a regimented one, and eventually the regimentation becomes unendurable or deadening. Pakistan has chosen to give itself strong medicine of the sort where an overdose can be fatal. It is not a case of kill or cure, but a case of throwing away the measuring spoon itself.

The euphoria of not having national destiny moulded in the matrix of Ittefaq foundry has had time to evaporate, yet we have not come to grips with the unreality of our present political state. General Musharraf's judgement has not let us down yet, but we cannot function as a selfrespecting nation without an objective system. The constitution may be in ambivalent abeyance, but what is active is one man's fiat and decisions.

Some functioning precautions have to be devised to prevent the National Security Council and its members from becoming unquestionable and unshakable oligarchs who legislate without reference to or in dissociation from the broader national fabric. Checks on the chief executive of our counter-coup and the council and cabinet through which he chooses to function and implement far-reaching policy decisions and daily administration have to be contrived. That is what legal expert should be considering before concentrating on a system for the future and the accountability of the past. We forget this need at our peril.

To be fair to go Gen. Musharraf, the hiatus that followed the counter-coup suggests he was trying to circumnavigate his way out of the crisis Mr. Sharif's conduct had precipitated without assuming civil and administrative authority himself. In the past, chiefs of army staff exercised decisive political influence behind the scene. But there was no initial conjunction of presidential or judical powers with the COAS at the expense of an uncertainly deposed prime minister. The parliament and other elements did not help him skate over the thin ice of the constitutionality that cracked.

Pragmatists now argue that the parliament is too large a body to be stage-managed, and that the majority of parliamentarians have a heavily vested interest in safeguarding party leaders and the former 'democratic' status quo on which they battened. Allowing a joint session of parliament is too much of a risk to the nationally welcomed Gen. Musharraf interregnum of systemic reform and accountability. Too embarrassing to be articulated is that most would condone a 'rigged' session of a parliament which guaranteed an indemnity to the counter-coup.

The prime minister's deposition was hailed for two broad reasons: national security was threatened by the collapse of the administrative structure and a calamitous depletion of the national economy combined with a mounting foreign debt. This same reason also makes it essential now to persuade creditors and donors not to penalise Pakistan for the events of October 12 and thereafter. Not wishing or able to live in isolation, Pakistan has to puzzle an acceptable way out of its bizarre political impasse.

The second reason for welcoming the counter-coup was that people feared Mr. Sharif's investing his office with dictatorial powers through the passage of the fifteenth constitutional amendment and the enfeeblement of the army high command. It would hardly serve popular purpose if citizens avoided one man's dictatorship only to accept another's.

However sound Gen. Musharraf's management might be, it brakes the momentum of growth towards responsible self-government. That is an evolutionary process and we have always lost faith in it along the way, resorting to radical treatment. It is important to retain continuity in the political process even while weeding it out.

Democracy's virtue in fact is that it exposes our deficiencies. It makes us face them till we learn how to banish them. Authoritarians and oligarchic systems leave us crippled with deficiencies and dependent on guides forever. The price of such guidance becomes civil liberties. Other options at this juncture include a national government that could also oversee elections under the system whose pros and cons we are familiar with, and where we can construct safeguards against the cons.

Thus, Gen. Musharraf would remain the caretaker chief executive and the NSC be included in the government. The conduct of the process of accountability for politicians and candidates would continue uninterrupted, entrusted to and supervised by those who have not been parliamentarians or served as their minions.

It the system to which people are to be elected is debated too long and democratic elections become too distant a goal, the lesson to remember from our past is not that distance lends enchantment but that distance leads away: compounding not resolving political problems.

Also in abeyance along with the constitution, and only in abeyance, are all the political ills from which the chief executive seeks to deliver the country and the people. But political disease cannot be treated when it is buried and kept under wraps. Nor can political practice be recast like a legal contract. The political system can only cure itself and politicians can only be reformed through the growing consciousness of a vigilant, involved public. The name for that process is democracy, and it is no sham.

---

* Courtesy : *The Pakistan Times,* November 16, 1999

13

In Search of Democracy

* *M.S. Qazi*

Chief Executive General Musharraf during his second leg of the three-state visit to Turkey, in reply to questions pertaining to spelling out a time-frame for return to democracy categorically stated that he was not in a position to give any time-frame, his aim was to bring Pakistan to a level it deserves and then he would 'silently withdraw' and finally civil rule would return after accomplishing the seven-point agenda. An analysis of his statement in the view of Pakistan's chequered political history during which the army intervened thrice (excluding present intervention) and ruled for 24 years is essential to put national affairs in right perspective.

Democracy is a way of governance. Its evolution takes decades. The evolution suffers if during the period of nurturing right type of leaders having vision, democratic instincts and temperament are not elevated to the helm of affairs by a popular vote.

Creation of Pakistan is a shinning example of democratic process. The struggle for the creation of Pakistan was led by the Quaid-i-Azam who beyond any shadow of doubt was a diehard democrat and profoundly committed to rule of law. He fought a constitutional battle and won Pakistan against insurmountable odds.

Subsequent to creation of Pakistan, luck did not favour her. First-line leaders who were to nurture roots of democracy in the newly born state, did not live longer. The PML which had certain inherent organisational deficiencies during pre-partition era but was compensated by strong democratic leadership of founding fathers failed to keep her democratic ethos and withered away within hardly a few years after partition because of intra-party fissures, self-serving leaders and strong interference by the civil and military bureaucracy who were waiting in the wings to set state affairs right in their misplaced and self-conviction.

The first organised effort was made by the army in 1958 who took over the reigns of power by abrogating 1956 constitution which the politicians had succeeded to make and implement after undergoing a hazardous constitutional making journey of approximately nine years. They were ill-prepared to build newly born state according to the democratic system they had inherited as the British legacy.

Ayub Khan who in 1958 led the military establishment to govern the country, did not pretend about his disliking for the western democracy. He stated in clear terms that the western parliamentary democracy even in its modified form did not suit the 'genius' of the Pakistani nation. Whether his remarks were apt or his wisdom was better than collective wisdom of mostly illiterate electorate who voted for creation of Pakistan, leaving these controversial points aside, his experiment to build state institutions through basic democracy did not succeed. Neither did his constitution succeed in short time-frame.

Ayub miserably failed to comprehend the essentials of nation building. Nations are hardly build through pre-set objectives without direct participation of the people at the grass-roots level. His four year martial law, six-year presidential rule with tacit support of defence services and well-executed decade of economic development which surely was a 'model' for other developing countries were like sand dooms because he did not nurture democracy and democratic institutions. His collapse and along with him collapse of state of Pakistan in 1971, had become obvious in 1969 when he handed over power to the army.

Yahya Khan, another representative of the military establishment tried to hold the state of Pakistan with the power of gun. His ill-conceived army action in former East Pakistan paved way for dismemberment of Pakistan.

After dismemberment of Pakistan, the country was put on the road to democracy by a populist leader, Zulfikar Ali Bhutto. He gave correct meaning to democracy which Ayub Khan and Yahya Khan had denied. It was empowering people. He succeeded to get 1973 Constitution approved by a parliament which comprised diverse political forces. It was certainly a great achievement. His slogan 'roti kapra aur makan' though misplaced, appealed to the psyche of the down-trodden millions. They took him for a messiah. He proved them wrong within short span of five years.

ZAB loved power like any leader does. He was averse to subjecting himself to democratic norms. He wanted to go down in history as a democrat who was committed to the cause of people yet he was unwilling to surrender his autocratic instincts and could not develop an urge in himself to build democratic institutions which the country urgently needed. Thin is where he went wrong. In 1977, people wanted him to go; he wanted to stick around at every cost. He even imposed selective martial law. Third party, the army, had to intervene for the third time with a limited agenda of holding elections within 90 days which stretched over to approximately 40-45 days. Abrupt end of Zia's 11-year-rule because of an air crash was a divine decision which brought back democracy to the country. It is to be appreciated that Zia during his life time had seen failure of his shoorabased system of governance and democracy got second life despite his aversion. He left behind a legacy of sectarianism, ethnicism and Kalashnikov culture.

After Zia the new populist leader was Benazir Bhutto. She had resolutely opposed Zia's dictatorial rule which he used to the hilt to crush the PPP but did not succeed. BB's rise to power was not undiluted. She had to operate within the constraints imposed by the army high Command. Article 58 2(b) which was inserted in the Constitution on Zia's insistence who had linked it with lifting martial law. The article was an additional constraint for her as she worked under the shadow of the army. The article empowered the president to dismiss the PM and her government if he was dissatisfied with the performance of the government. BB was dismissed twice and Nawaz Sharif was dismissed once. Second time, he landed in greater trouble in a tussle for power which got intensified after the negative fallout of the Kargil conflict.

Nawaz Sharif during his second stint of owner failed to deliver the results as he and Benazir had failed earlier. He succeeded to bring all state institutions, executive, parliament, judiciary under his control and tried to muzzle the press also. Exit of former COAS General Karamat after he had voiced his opinion about deterioration of state institutions and proposed to establish National Security Council to over-see the state affairs, sent a clear signal about the absolute power which the former PM had gained and the democracy despite having all institutions intact did not have any substance. He was certainly nurturing a sham and hollow democracy.

Pakistan's search for democracy through civilian and military establishment is a story of unsuccessful experimentation; the selfserving leaders empowered themselves and weakened state and democratic institutions. Ayub Khan's basic democracy, Yahya Khan's democracy through barrel of the gun, Zia's shoora-cracy and politicians' (ZAB, BB and Nawaz Sharif) sham and hollow democracy were in fact misplaced attempts to fool the masses.

The CE has vowed to usher an era of 'true' and 'strong' democracy before handing over power to the civilians. History is on record that all military rulers of Pakistan and of other countries also made a similar start yet they ended up in prolonging their stay in power and had to quit unwillingly. The agendas they had set themselves were not radically different from the Musharraf's agenda. The conclusion should not elude any one.

The civil-military setup now being experimented is not sustainable to govern the nation in a democratic mould. If history and experience are any guide, the CE should pay heed to the suggestion given to him by the president and prime minister of Turkey. They have experienced the best and worst of civil-military relations till this day to manage the state affairs. Their suggestion to the CE to return to democracy, howsoever flawed it might be, should carry a lot of weight. The new setup should set limited targets of restoring the economy, retrieving the looted national wealth and containing corruption. Two-three years' time should be the maximum timeframe after which the military leaders should make it mandatory for themselves to return to barracks. That is the best option for them as well as for the nation.

---

* Courtesy : *The Pakistan Times,* November 16, 1999

14

Democracy's Failure

* *Brig (Rtd.) M. Abdul Hafiz*

Barkhurdar, mujhe khauf to ye hai ke Kuchh bhi nahi hoga./ Aise hi chalta rahega.

(Youngman, my fear is that nothing will happen./Things ill continue the way the are.)

Faiz Ahmed Faiz

So said Pakistan's unrecognised poet-laureate of the country's off-and-on crises bringing the nation on the brink. What he said reflected both a measure of cynicism in the mood and the nation's unlimited tenacity for survival under any circumstances. As Pakistan is gripped with another crisis with an unceremonious halt of democracy and universally condemned military takeover, the poet's prophetic verdict is apparently under test. Can Pakistan, with her enormous predicaments, still continue the way it is? A baffled world community aptly look askance. While a new wave of cynicism sweeps the country, the doomsayers' prognosis is that of an impending doom.

Surprisingly, however, the furors over Pakistan's democratic setback rages everywhere except in Pakistan where its people are strangely enamoured with their men in uniform. When the country's first coup took place exactly 41 years ago on 8 October

1958 there were jubilations in the streets hailing the military as the nation's saviour. Afterwards anytime the military seized power in Pakistan the public reaction has invariably been one of awe and admiration. Each time it stepped in—the takeover went in a textbook manner without any one faltering at any point. This time the coup looked even more spontaneous with the troops taking their battle locations without a declared leader. And none from among the public went berserk with his love for democracy!

The syndrome is not without reasons. The Pakistanis living under military and quasi-military rules for most time of their existence hardly tasted anything new when on 12 October last General Pervaiz Musharraf, Pakistan's army chief, dismissed the elected government of Nawaz Sharif and declared himself the country's chief executive. Because neither the government of Sharif nor that of Benazir Bhutto before him was much dissimilar in their harshness from any earlier military government. While Sharif had been the product of Zia's regime, Bhutto's father and mentor came into political limelight as the 'whiz kid' of Ayub Khan's martial law cabinet. None of them was nourished in the traditions of democracy and could abide by its norm. On the other hand, Bhutto combined in herself a kind of feudal arrogance and an appetite for money and Sharif showed callous indifference to public agony while building up his family's business empire.

A decade-long experimentation since General Zia's death in 1988 air crash the process was not only interrupted by frequent intervenation, the power was divided among the president, prime minister and the military through the stipulations of the constitution's 8th amendment. The relations between the president and the prime minister remained most acrimonious during all the regimes. The parliament and the office of the prime minister was made subservient to a presidency strengthened during the Zia regime. The prime minister was always hemmed in by the advice of the army chief on one hand and by the president on the other in a typical power-sharing arrangement by so called 'troika'.

With heavy electoral mandate in 1997 Sharif was able to dilute this arrangement through 13th amendment and take away much of the president's discretionary power. But Leghari continued to act like an executive president treating himself as moral and political arbiter of the nation. The same went for the prestige and influence of army chief in spite of his repeated avowals of being only a subordinate component of the government. Later, in a bitter power struggle when Sharif established the parliament's supremacy he himself became a monster of power and behaved like a despot. His conduct and dispensation in governance became indistinguishable from those of military dictators. His dependence more on the cabal and sychopants took away the essence of the democracy marking the beginning of an end of his moral authority.

There are also historical as well as socio-political factors which make Pakistan's transition from a feudal entity to modern democracy a difficult proposition. During the colonial period, the British nourished only the regulated presidencies of India i.e. Bengal, Bombay and Madras, the earliest British possessions on the sub-continent for democracy and rule of law. In a medieval semi-feudal system in the western region having the shortest exposure to British rule the people living there were not considered even for the grant of fundamental rights. This partly explains why the common men in Pakistan are politically less conscious and interested, giving military its clout and primacy. Only 35 percent of the electorate voted in 1997 election in which Sharif won with overwhelming majority.

In this socio-political milieu which prevails till now, the politics in Pakistan is the preserve of the feudal elite and now burgeoning business magnets as well as industrial barons comprising more of less 300 families. Through blood ties, marriages and business links they dominate the military, the bureaucracy and the government. There is not much of an urban middle class considered essiental for parliamentary democracy of which Pakistan is one of the three practitioners in the Muslim world – the others being Bangladesh and Malaysia.

Pakistan by choice embarked at its independence on a difficult course of parliamentary democracy with the temperament that suited only an authoritarian rule. Small wonder that henceforth the power changed hands only among imperious politicians, military brass and wily bureaucrats supported by businessmen and industrialists. But they all behaved in the same manner whether it was Ghulam Muhammad, Iskander Mirza, Ayub Khan, ZA Bhutto, Ziaul Huq or Nawaz Sharif—although they functioned under different political dispensation. It was a foregone conclusion that the military would clamp down in the situation that was prevailing prior to Musharraf's putsch. Even the United States warned of it sufficiently ahead of time. Yet it could not be forestalled.

Because the nations have their own internal dynamics which propel them in certain directions, neither the domestic authority nor the external arbiters of moral standard can do much about it. While Pakistan's new ruler gives indications of a long haul before democracy can be restored in the country, an outraged international community has reacted sharply to the change. The major powers have warned Pakistan of various punitive steps to be taken against her. The British Commonwealth of nations has suspended Pakistan from the organisation. The international financial organisations give indications of more stringent dealing with Pakistan. The US has also announced a stoppage of arms sale to her longtime ally.

Much of these reactions of the external powers and agencies are presumably aimed at discouraging prolonged military rule in Pakistan. They otherwise know that they cannot reverse the process in another country just by showing their anger and pushing the offending regime to a diplomatic isolation. The countries which were annoyed with the military regime in Myanmar in the aftermath of its clamp-down on the pro-democracy demonstrators in 1989 and setting aside the election results in 1990 gradually reconciled with the status quo in Myanmar. While paying lip-service to democracy and human rights in public, the US also has been quietly carrying on business with Myanmar in spite of its almost four decades of military rule. Because she is prepared to give the turf exclusively to China which has already made significant inroads into Myanmar.

After the Cold War, although there was triumph for democracy and liberal politics in many countries, the military continues to assert itself as support base and often as political arbiter where democracy is yet to strike firm roots. These days it has become fashionable to have a democratic set-up whatever may be its content under the outer garb. The democracy's failures to meet the people's aspirations and material needs catalysed a series of military coups during the fifties and sixties. Given the way democracy has been functioning and faltering in many developing countries, the return of another wave of militarism can hardly be ruled out. The fear that a military regime would lose its external patrons has never been substantiated. So long such a regime serves the strategic and other purposes of the big powers, it hardly matters what is its hue. More so for Pakistan which still holds promises and potential for recovery. It seems prudent to keep her constructively engaged. Amidst a spate of initial outburst against the change in Pakistan, the United States keeps options open for engaging Pakistan.

In a strategic region in the fringes of both South West Asia and Central Asia, no world power can afford to abandon Pakistan and let it slide away to opposite camp—particularly at a time when a new international power balance has been shaping up. It is true that Pakistan needs a total overhaul of its society and polity with sweeping reforms before its people can shake off their cynicism over the country's future, but she is certainly not confronted with an immediate doom.

---

* Courtesy : *The Frontier Post (Pakistan),* November 30, 1999

15

The Democratic Dilemma

** A.A. Musalman*

The second Nawaz government has been 'dismissed' by the army unlike Junejo, Benazir and first Nawaz governments which were all dismissed by the president under the authority of now-defunct Article-58 (2) (b) of the Constitution and not by the army. There is as such no paralled between the present and the earlier-quoted dismissals. The only parallel in the 'new' Pakistan is that of the dismissal of ZAB by Zia ul Haq on the 5th of July 1977.

In the 'original' Pakistan, the 1958 martial law overthrew a government that could not, in any way, be classed as an 'elected', government. In 1969 Ayub Khan himself violated his own constitution by handing over power to the commander-in-chief instead to the speaker of the National Assembly as was provided for the transfer in the constitution. All of Yahya's action were as such ab initio without legal authority. In any case Ayub Khan's Basic Democracy-based regime cannot be, in any sense, termed as an 'elected' regime in the sense 'democracy' is spoken of.

The present action of the army can only be thus compared to that of Zia against ZAB because ZAB also carried 'unprecedented' mandate in the 1977 election disputed by the main opposition PNA on charges of 'rigging'. The same is the case with the 'unprecedentedly mandated' Nawaz regime who also carried the 'rigging' charge levelled by main opposition PPP in the 1997 elections. The decision of the Supreme Court in the Nusrat Bhutto case is, therefore, the only grund norm on which the present action of the army chief can be examined for its legal validity and constitutional cover. The decision in this case not only validated the action of the army chief but also granted him the power to amend the Constitution with the condition that elections must be held as early as possible.

The demise of the supposedly 'heavily mandated' regime to almost universal rejoicing and relief of the people is proof enough to validate the army action because no other constitutional course is presently available to remove a highly recalcitrant PM and his most unpopular regime. An ordinary citizen is bewildered at the unwillingness of the armed forces to clamp martial law in the present scenario for which they have the necessary legal sanction in order to enable the chief executive to amend the Constitution in a way so that this unfortunate country is rid of the present system of 'democracy' that in a single decade has through lawlessness, aggrandisement and corruption brought it near complete political, moral and financial ruin. Elections then can be held under the new system after cleansing all the rubbish that has made political governance of Pakistan sorely stink.

Any system of governance must work to the benefit of the country and its people. It must, per force, suit the pysche of the people and conform to their traditions and history. Muslims have no history of parliamentary democracy of Whitehall type, which also does not suit their pysche. For people who do not separate religion from state, like the Muslims, morality takes precedence over majority because moral conduct is an built-in virtue based on belief, whereas majority can be contrived through various means.

This one conflict of parliamentary democracy with Islamic norms is vividly pointed out by Allama Iqbal in the famous verse 'Jamhoriat ek tarze hakumat hai ke jisman/Bandoon ko gina kerta hain tola nahen karta'. The meaning and spirit of democracy is that the ruler has consent of the ruled. It is not necessary that this can be done only via parliamentary system which in effect is an indirect system of electing the chief executive. Compared to this is the presidential system in which the chief executive is directly elected by the people and in essence is the system preferred by Islam as practised during the Caliphate through the medium of open 'bayat'. In this system of election the chief executive is elected directly by the general masses or the Ummah instead of limited numbers in the elected assemblies. The choice in this case shall as such be much more broadly based and depend on personal qualities.

The biggest flaw of parliamentary system is that in it the executive is not separate from the legislature and thus permits biggest of the perfidies to be legitimised through a process of law in the name of democracy by way of the tyranny of brute or contrived majority in the legislature. The recent 'decade of democracy' is the worst living example of such a scenario with Benazir bowing to basest wishes of her own and of a contrived majority and Nawaz Sharif ruling like a monarch on the basis of a brute majority.

The third dimension of this paradox is the Indian example where three general elections had to be held for lack of majority for a single political party. It is for the Indians to sort out their issue but for Pakistan the system of parliamentary democracy has proved to be the root cause of all ills of governance and malpractices of all kinds prevalent unchecked in society. The foremost necessity is to replace the present system with directly elected presidential system. Example of Ayub's system with its negative fallout are given but Ayub's was a quai-dictatorship of restricted franchise of vested interests and not in any means any type of directly elected presidential system. A successful system must conform to realities.

The 'original' as well as 'amended' 1973 Constitution has following flaws:

(1) A 'ceremonial' Senate with no effective say in the affairs of the federation.

This is against the very concept of the federalism particularly in a country like Pakistan where one federating unit outnumbers all other put together.

(2) An 'emasculated' judiciary subject to manipulation by the executive.

(3) A 'bonded' Parliament with members 'throttled' and subject to arbitrary unseating as also hijacking and detention to prevent assembly sessions.

(4) Absence of any meaningful checks and balances and with the emergency provisions suited more to political requirements of the ruling elite rather than the security and safety of the country.

It is a matter of profound regret that such infirmities in the Constitution were wilfully planted by all those who authored it as well as those who came to amend it in order to serve their ambitions and agendas. The results of such perverted actions are before everybody.

In view of aforesaid 'flaws', the following amendments to the suspended Constitution are suggested to remove various anomalies, specially the grievances of smaller units.

(a) Clause-(3) of Article-41 be subsituted as follows:

"Election to the office of president shall be held in a manner similar to election to the members of the National Assembly in all constituencies and result declared on the basis of total number of votes cast in favour of each candidate in all of NA constituencies in a province multiplied by smallest number of National Assembly seats in a province for the time being and divided by total number of seats in the National Assembly including those of minorities and women. Votes of each candidate in all of the provinces calculated as above shall then be totalled and the one with the highest number of votes shall be declared successful provided these votes are not less than 51% of the total vote cast failing that a runoff election shall be held between two candidates with highest votes.

Article-7 and Articles-46 to 48 along with the Second Schedule, be deleted. Articles-91 to 95 be deleted and a Clause-(3) be added to Article-90 with the provision that "the president will appoint a council of ministers, advisers and special assistants in order to aid and advise him in exercise of his functions which will be responsible to the president but the total strength of this council shall not exceed 10% of the total strength of Parliament at any given time. If any member of Parliament is appointed to this council, such member will have to vacate the seat of Parliament before taking a seat in the council of ministers of president.

(b) Having separated the legislature from the executive, it is necessary to insulate its members from the coercive powers of the executive and to enable it to act as a 'check' without any fear of dissolution. Most effective 'check' is through financial control since money makes the mare go. To this end, the suggested amendments are:

(i) Deletion of Article-58 and the words 'unless sooner dissolved' from Article-52.

(ii) The executive shall ensure attendance of all sesseions by any member detained for the time being under any law whether arrested before or during a session.

(iii) Abolishing the 14th Amendment except in case of floor crossing.

(iv) Repealing the Eighth and 13th Amendments.

(v) Restraining the executive from any expenditures outside budget and from incurring other financial liabilities before prior sanction of the Parliament. All schemes of sale or transfer of public assets shall require prior approval of Parliament.

(c) In any meaningful federal set-up, the Senate or the House of Federation is the key to ensure equality of all units in federal affairs irrespective of population, resources and size of individual unit. This is the only way of ensuring national integreation and of avoiding any sense of deprivation and alienation in the federal system. This aspect is totally lacking in the current scheme of things and is the reason all talk of confederation. The status and power of the Senate as at present needs to enhanced by investing it with:

(i) Powers to approve all money bills including the budget after its approval by the National Assembly where all such measures shall be initiated by the president.

(ii) Exclusive power to ratify treaties and accept contracts with foreign countries.

(iii) Final authority to appoint, transfer and remove judges of the Supreme and High Courts, CEC and members of the Election Commission and the auditor general.

(d) In order to make the legislature attend its primary function of law-making, presidential power to issue ordinances (Article-89) shall be abolished and instead the president shall be empowered to request Parliament for emergency legislation whenever such a need arises. Moreover the president shall be granted the power to veto bills presented for assent with the proviso that such votes can be overridden by Parliament with 2/3 vote.

(e) The constitutional set-up in the provinces shall be mutatus mutandis—the same as at federal level.

(f) Article-232 shall be limited to issuing emergency proclamation for whole of the country and its application to any one province be deleted for which Articel-234 only should be used with prior conset of the Senate.

(g) All land in private ownership should be resumed to the state in accordance with the decision of Hazrat Umar (RA) and contracted out to sitting tenents on favourable terms. The Islamic levy of Ushr be compulsorily collected by provincial governments to greatly widen the provincial resources. According to available data it is estimated to yield 25 billion rupees. The federal government shall divest collection and utilisation of Zakat to provinces as an item of provincial budget and not according to present Zakat Councils. The collection and utilisation of sales tax be given to provinces and with it the federal divisable pool abolished.

Finally, a word about the clamour for restoring 'democracy'. People agree to be ruled willingly according to the terms and conditions settled in a Social Contract called the Constitution and it is no use having a Constitution without constitutionalism. That is rank hypocrisy and Allah Almighty admonishes hypocrites in gravest terms and promises harshest punishments hereinafter. Islam's greatest emphasis is on justice and beneficience. Allah Almighty curses liars in no uncertain terms (Lanalt Allahe al-al kazibeen) and abhors tyranny most candidly (In Allah la Uhib az-zalimeen). Unfortunately, these traits are the hallmark of the politics in the so-called parliamentary democracy as practised in the Islami Republic of Pakistan by all those crying for its return for selfaggrandisement.

---

* Courtesy : *The Frontier Post,* October,20,1999

16

Democracy Blues

** Mir Jamilur Rahman*

The rabbit was running at breakneck speed. The fox stopped him to inquire, "Are you OK? why such haste?" The rabbit answered in a shaken voice; "Don't you know. The Lion King has decided to eat animals that have small ears." "Well, that should not worry you," the fox said patronisingly, "Anybody can see you have large ears." The rabbit explained, "You are right, but there is a problem. The Lion King would check the ear size after he has eaten the animal."

That was exactly what the State Bank did. It froze the bank accounts of all the 'notable' politicians including their spouses and children. Even the president was not spared. The Senate chairman, who is a heartbeat away from the presidency, was given the same treatment. After having discomforted and dishonoured thousands of account holders, including some dead, the State Bank has now started measuring their 'notability'. It has restored the accounts of those 'notables' who are not loan defaulters. The State Bank should have taken this precaution before freezing the accounts and not after the freeze.

A year and a half ago the State Bank of Pakistan had won universal recognition as the 'Master Freezer' by freezing the forex accounts. It was the mother of all freezes for it had led to the freezing of government creditability. The thousands of depositors, majority of them from overseas, are still wondering where their 11 billion dollars have gone. The CBR is also apt in freezing bank accounts, especially those held by the nonconformist press. The Jang Group has gone through this ordeal and the Friday Times is experiencing it.

The National Security Council is complete, but the federal cabinet is still short of ten ministers. The chief executive has taken great care in choosing his men and yet some of his nominations have come under fire. It was but natural because it would be impossible to achieve 100 per cent consensus on every nominee. However, these nominations show that age and experience have gained importance. Nawaz Sharif had offered discounted airfares to senior citizens while Gen. Musharraf has inducted them in the government.

Gen. Musharraf's cabinet would be composed of technocrats and specialists. Unlike a political head, his choice of ministers would not be dictated by political, regional or ethnic considerations. Obviously he is looking for the best and the most honest among us but it is not clear what method he has adopted to judge the calibre and honesty of the candidates. Perhaps it is done like this. First, somebody proposes a name as Imran Khan has claimed to have done. Second, the name is sent to the intelligence to check the antecedents. Finally the chief executive interviews him/her and makes up his mind.

This method of selection could be improved upon by widening the field of choice. The best and the honest may escape the attention of the chief executive if the selection of the ministers was restricted to proposals received from here and there. An administrative genius or a financial wizard buried in his assignment somewhere in the world may not be aware that Pakistan is looking for a man like him.

The objective of finding the best could be achieved by advertising the ministerial posts. As our preference is for technocrats and specialists, therefore it should not be difficult to set the eligibility parameters for the candidates. Among other qualifications like education and experience, it may also be added that applicants should be 70 years old or above. Experience of working in the IMF or the World Bank would be desirable. Holders of a character certificate from the State Department would get preference.

It is not a farfetched idea considering that when we need an efficient stenographer we advertise for it. The ministerial assignment is much more important and carries heavier responsibilities than a lowly stenographer. Therefore, it would not be out of place to invite applications for the cabinet and other key posts.

Some eyebrows have been raised at the suspension of parliament and provincial assemblies. However, the PML legislators are hardly in a position to object to the suspension. Did they object when their leader suspended the Sindh Assembly? Some of them are now criticising Nawaz Sharif for his autocratic way of governance. But it is tantamount to crying over spilt milk. Did they make any serious efforts to stop the speedy passage of the constitutional amendments 13 and 14 giving dictatorial powers to Nawaz Sharif? Their public criticism of these measures might have deterred Nawaz Sharif from following a suicidal course. Now it is too late. In fact, the people hardly miss the National Assembly because its cringing members had made it a rubberstamp.

The evil deeds have the bad habit of visiting upon its perpetrator as is evident from the demand that Nawaz Sharif should be tried in a military court. Mr. Nawaz Sharif was the great exponent of speedy justice and had special courts established for that purpose. The saner element advised against it, but Nawaz Sharif would not listen. He may soon get a taste of his own medicine. However, that would not serve the cause of justice. If he is accused of any crime, the trial should be held in a normal court and under normal laws. A speedy trial under special laws would leave many doubts here and abroad.

Nawaz Sharif and his minister of information hated the Human Rights Commission of Pakistan (HRCP) for questioning the human rights violations. The HRCP condemned the so-called police encounters and the strong-arm tactics against the independent press. Inronically, the HRCP is the solitary voice that has demanded Nawaz Sharif's release. The HRCP has asked the government either to free him or take him to the court.

Mr. Hussain Nawaz in London has protested against the media trial of his father. The protest sounds familiar. Not long ago Benazir Bhutto used to protest for the same reason. But there is a big difference between the two hatchet jobs. The one against Benazir Bhutto was conducted on the government controlled PTV. In the case of Nawaz Sharif it is only confined in the independent press. The government is keeping clear of making wild accusations against him.

Mushahid Hussain Syed was the second most publicised man in the realm. PTV, radio and the press would give him projection second only to Nawaz Sharif. Sadly, nobody has spoken for him. Let me cast the first stone by asking for his freedom. All his colleagues have been released, his team of scoundrels is roaming free but he is still in protective custody and incommunicado. That is not fair.

---

* Courtesy : *The Pakistan Times,* November 4, 1999

17

The Paradox of Democracy in Pakistan

** Shamila N. Chaudhary*

While the Unites States is calling for a swift return to democracy in Pakistan, popular support in Pakistan remains steadfast in its belief that military control is beneficial in order to address the shortterm problems plaguing the nation. Although the idea of a military coup may seem daunting and oppressive to those living in countries with democracies, the army is the most organised and disciplined institution in Pakistan that has the capacity to initiate and mandate immediate necessities and structural changes necessary to facilitate the future emergence of democracy. By taking care of the immediate needs and following through on the key points proposed in General Pervaiz Musharraf's first public speech, the transition government in Pakistan will lay the groundwork for democracy in Pakistan's future.

When the United States called for an immediate and swift return to democracy days after the coup, the irony of its statement was obvious. Looting millions while in power, both Nawaz Sharif and Benazir Bhutto pursued personal and political party ambitions instead of sufficiently addressing issues of sectarian violence, human resource development and poverty. Surely, this is not the form of democracy the US would like Pakistan to return to.

While the Pakistani government has had public elections in the past 11 years, fulfilling democracy's procedural obligation, elected officials still failed to provide the people with substantive forms of democratic governance. By calling for a swift return to democracy, the US focuses more on the need for a procedural form of democracy than an actual substantive one. The question remains, if the procedures of democracy failed to produce a substantive democracy in Pakistan, then what can?

General Pervaiz Musharraf told reporters in his first news conference that members of the suspended parliament were not the true representatives, and I want to give real democracy to the people. Elected officials were essentially the same people, looters of national wealth, with different faces. Establishing a real democracy entails both eliminating the culture of corruption which plagues Pakistani politics and reviving the faltering economy. Before all other issues, these are the foremost needs of the nation.

Having a long history in Pakistan, both corruption and the faltering economy appear inextricable. However, change and progress are possible given Musharraf's creation of the National Accountability Bureau (NAB). If NAB follows through on its mission, it will hold looters and loan defaulters accountable, bringing back the much-needed money plundered by politicians, bureaucrats, and businesspeople. NAB is one of many structural changes attempting to establish economic and political stability in Pakistan.

Thus, the military coup emerged in response to a dire situation in which Pakistan's experiment with democracy was failing. Herein lies the paradox of democracy in Pakistan: in order for substantive democracy to thrive, the procedures of democracy must be temporarily eliminated. J. Samuel Fitch writes in "*Armies and Politics in Latin America 1975-1985*":

"Coups occur when military officers believe a crisis situation exists. Public disorders and public opinion hostile to the government, threats to the military's institutional interests, violations of the constitutions by civilian presidents, evident inability of the incumbent administration to manage a serious economic crisis will increase the military's sense of crisis, Personal ambitions and personal ties may influence individual officers, but the decision to stage a military coup is generally an institutional decision, reflecting the collective evaluation of government performance within the upper ranks of the armed forces as a whole."

Some have said that the military coup was spurred by Musharraf's personal ambition since Sharif had replaced Musharraf with General Khawaja Ziauddin as chairman of Joint Chiefs of Staff Committee (JCSC) and Chief of the Army Staff shortly before the coup. Although personal ambition does play a small factor, as J. Samuel Fitch argues, the greater emphasis should be placed on Musharraf's removal as an extension of Sharif's attempts to politicise the army by placing supporters of his policies in all positions of authority. Sharif's attempts are just more examples of poor government performance while Musharraf's coup counters Sharif's deplorable democracy by dismantling it and attempting to address immediate economic and political necessities through structural changes. Amongst the main economic and political necessities being addressed, Musharraf's first speech to the Pakistani people introduced other points of focus for the transition government. Some significant points are: (1) the devolution of power to the people, as envisioned in the Constitution, (2) freedom of the press and the establishment of private television and radio stations, (3) reject elements that spread hatred and violence, and (4) safeguarding the rights of minorities.

These points lay the groundwork for a potential emergence of both substantive and procedural forms of democracy in Pakistan. These points deal with the more substantive issues of democracy and must be executed alongside the procedural aspects. However, these points are obviously more difficult in nature to establish in comparison to locating loan defaulters or holding looters accountable. Bureaus and committees addressing sectarian violence and freedom of speech can always be formed and exist in name. But to effectively produce democracy, something more must be done. The mentality and attitudes of the Pakistani public in relation to these issues must be addressed. To do this requires time and new ways of approaching controversial and problematic issues. For this reason, a small one among many, Pakistan cannot currently declare a state of democracy.

A true democracy is a government by the people implemented directly or through the procedures of elected representation. It considers the common people as the primary source of power. Its substantive nature advocates principles of social equality and individual rights. Musharraf speaks of the importance of social equality and the need to consider the common people when he says, "Tell the poor we will always stand by them. Tell the rich: stop bleeding this country. Stop your corruption. It is time for us to come together to rebuild Pakistan. In order for the Pakistani people to rebuild Pakistan together, they must see each other as equals. The common people must be given power."

For Pakistan to ever see this type of democracy, many obstacles have to be overcome, more than merely economic and political. The 'restoration' of democracy in Pakistan will be neither swift nor simple. Nevertheless, for the paradox of democracy in Pakistan to establish democracy as a reality, democracy must be restored based on the timetable of the country it is sorely needed in.

---

* Courtesy : *The Frontier Post, (Pakistan),* November 23, 1999

18

The Coup Must Usher in Long-Due Purge

* *Nisar Ahmad*

In the political underworld of Pakistan, majority of our politicians can be branded as hypocrites and manipulative who are ever ready to play for audience different jingles, suiting the moment, and practise all peppery tactics during elections for seducing voters and seizing the power. Once in power, for these politicians all virtues of character, intelligence, capability or any other markings that are imperative for good governance obviously remain inapplicable. And unfortunately this has been the tradition of our socalled democratic system since the inception of our country where, consequently, we never had a chance to hammer out the essentials to gradually establish a true form of democracy, as the neighbouring India has.

Tragically, on few occasions when we desired to initiate the long and difficult process of estabilshing this true form of democracy, we rather experienced a series of transpositions between military dictatorship and civilian autocracy. In both cases however, the land barons, feudal lords and their agents in civil and military bureaucracies always blocked and tackled our path. They continued playing as members of the nobility as if they have the divine right to rule the country and plunder its wealth. Not only that but, because of the inbred disloyalty of these forces to the country, they would lease out our homeland to foreign powers in order to promote and facilitate their gameplans in the region. And this sellout has been done for the price of peanuts that instead of enriching the country's economy, was usually put to use to buttress their own grip on power.

It was not unexpected that the end of another such dysfunctional democracy under Nawaz Sharif earned applauds from populace at large. All quarters of the society including the most liberal democrats in the country, have hailed the military takeover. Not out of love for the military rule, of course, but for their abhorrence for Nawaz Sharif's civilian dictatorship that was getting worse with each passing day. In the past two years and half the deposed prime minister's practices and manners served as yet another lesson to the public that democracy as an institution does not yet exist in Pakistan and whatever hodgepodge we experience as democracy is in fact efforts of depredation among these political riff-raffs in disguise.

Nawaz Sharif himself topped the list of those dirty froths as the most ingenious impersonator and talented liar of our short democratic history. Behind his soft voice and baby face, Nawaz was able to cloak the most ghastly elements of greed and deceit, which seemed ingrained in his self-seeking personality. Taking cover behind people's verdict, he appeared unfettered to create a vast domain of cronies and corrupts to promote his underhand deals that netted him and his coteries billions. Punjab became another name for Pakistan. To build and develop only the constituencies of his supporters, the legitimate rights of the people in the rest of the three provinces were violated and betrayed. Thus tampering with the foundation on which the survival of the federation rests its premises continued in many forms.

The former chief minister of Punjab, Shahbaz Sharif, travelled around the world to solicit foreign investment to develop and modernise localities in Punjab only. This manoeuvre might have comforted his political loyalists, but certainly boosted antagonism and sedition among the people of other provinces against Punjab. As a paranoid leader, Nawaz tried to seize control of every institution in the country that made him feel secure. Similarly, he persisted on taking control of all provincial governments with the aim of extending and perpetuating his grip on power. In one such case, after betraying the ANP on agreements that led to its break-up of alliance with the PML(N), Nawaz, without encumbrance, spent hundreds of millions of the nation's wealth on buying provincial member's loyalities to retain the government, making democracy a laughing stock.

He perpetrated the extreme crime against the federation by attempting to sow the seeds of discord among army generals and undermining the judiciary. He initiated conspiracies to disgrace the army by putting a price tag on army generals and commanders. The aim was to secure himself while depriving the nation of the vitality of the only viable institution in the country that we turn to, in times of crisis. The former chief of army staff Gen. Karamat was pressured, put down, heckled and finally forced out, much to the contempt of the armed forces and the nation. The case of former chief justice Sajjad Ali Shah became a classic example of Nawaz's pranks in which the chief justice was targeted for harassment and when he refused to compromise the integrity of his insitution, was ousted.

Acting in the manner of an emperor, Nawaz rarely considered of any importance, visits to parliamentary sessions but nevertheless used his two-thirds majority in the assembly, whenever necessary, to amend the Constitution to augment his control and authority to be a real dictator. If on one side he was pressuring banks to arrange loans to his political cronies, on the other he organised mob attack on the Supreme Court to deny judges the records of his corruption in the past. Playing oppressive and divisive politics, promoting religious extremism, and stirring the embers of discard among the military commanders, all these Nawaz government's escapades were serving blows directly at the very foundation of the federation.

Instead of seeing the opposition as an essential part of the democratic process, a primary force that helps create balance and stability in a democratic setup, he treated it as an adversary that must be eradicated at any cost. Every time he acted, the aim seemed to be personal profit and political gains and the result was further undercutting the democracy and weakening the civic institutions whose integrity, to an elected leader, should be as important as the physical borders of the country. These sorts of demeanor alone brought to light Nawaz government's ineptness and inefficiency that made his fall from power as the cause for celebration among the public.

Nawaz Sharif was responsible for the Kargil crisis that brought India and Pakistan on the verge of another bloody war but when the affair turned out to be a misadventure, he simply propagated it as the work of the COAS Gen. Musharraf. The world media picked on this theme and major powers by common consent believed that the Pakistan Army was to blame as the main troublemaker in Kargil. With all this dressing down of the army, a period of suspicion between Nawaz Sharif and Gen. Musharraf ensued, raising Nawaz's feeling of vulnerability to new heights as his design called for absolute power at any cost.

Under the circumstances, the chief executive's announcement in September that he will not retire before the end of his tenure next year in October left Nawaz under no illusion that Musharraf had revolved from being a partner to an obstacle. In the past among other supportive gestures, the army had helped recover WAPDA dues and over looked Nawaz misuse of anti-terrorists act to harass political opposition. But now his unrestrained pilferage schemes of national exchequer and political shell games, with Musharraf as COAS, seemed risky.

A decision was made to replace Mushrarraf with ISI's Gen. Ziauddin who, in Washington, had pledged fidelity to track the course as Uncle Same commanded for curbing domestic religious extremism" and the spread of "terrorism" from across the border in Afghanistan. An era of new allegiance to the old master was to begin shortly. Before setting a trap to eradicate Musharraf's threat, Nawaz erroneously thought he already had split the army top cadre to his benefit, but his October 12 strike against Musharraf boomeranged, that for the time being, also proved a setback to American plans.

People have welcomed Gen. Pervaiz Musharraf's takeover because their faith in the country's politicians has shattered repeatedly. In the past 14 years we have seen five civilian governments that failed to deliver. This euphoria about military government is ominous because we know that in the past great damage to the country's institutions was brought about by military dictators. But this time around the infant democracy was let down, dishonoured and scandalised, supposedly, by its protector. The nation trusted Nawaz to build up and make democracy work but he deviated from the course and rendered it insolvent. The nation felt relieved when the army finally decided to be done with him.

There are no simplistic answers on how to build up a workable democracy and cure the ailing economy but we have to set out to realise these goals eventually. Now is the right time. The current military regime does not seem to have political ambitions and the post Cold War era is, anyhow, discouraging for military dictators. The animosity with India must not go or forever. Rapprochement between the two will allow us to cut the number of our armed forces and divert resources from military use (currently 1/3 of the total budget) to civilian economy. Recovery of all loans from defaulters and accountability of corrupt leaders with permanent disqualification from politics of guilty politician will serve as an example for the aspiring leaders.

Concrete steps towards: 1) abolishing the feudal system by gradual extensive land reforms and 2) breaking the grip of these few feudal families on our political parties are inevitable if Gen. Musharraf wants to bring change. People can wait for 10 years for an election to take place if they see progress being made in the right direction under military/civilian partnership government.

---

* Courtesy : *The Frontier Post (Pakistan),* October 28, 1999

19

A Bitter Harvests and New Beginnings

* *Shafqat Mahmood*

The military takeover on October 12 was unexpected. I am convinced that had Nawaz Sharif not tried to engineer a coup within the army, this would never have happened. From what we can now tell, the armed forces had serious reservations about Sharif's style of governance. They were also alarmed by his repeated attempts to create groups and divide the senior leadership of the military. Yet it seems they were determined to respond only to the extent of protecting their institution from political interference and no more. Taking over of the government was never on the cards. Mr. Nawaz Sharif forced them to it.

No one, least of all the military, are ecstatic about this turn of events. A heavy responsibility has been placed on their shoulders. Pakistan truly is in a mess. The structure of governance is in shambles. The economy is going through the worst recession in our history. The state is practically bankrupt with expenses soaring to over 700 billion rupees and the income only 300 billion. Thanks to the Sharif's foreign policy we have never been more isolated in the world. These are not easy times for our country and now the burden, the cares and the responsibility to steer us out of this quagmire has passed on to the military.

They will do their duty and they will do it as well as they can but it will not be easy. There probably are no elaborate plans in place because there was no plan to take over. This message has come through loud and clear not only to us but to the international community. Comments in the British and the American press, under no compulsion to play politics, testify to this. It will therefore be some time before the contours of a new policy pakcage for the country become visible.

One thing is clear, though. Having been reluctantly pushed into civilian affairs, the military seems determined to do its duty and not pass on the buck to a ragtag, quickly cobbled together government. Friday's announcement of the provisional constitutional order is a testimony to that. Had General Musharraf wanted to take a backseat, he would have tried to engineer an in-house change. We would have then been stuck with the same old reviled faces. He has chosen not to do that and thank god for that. If circumstances and the will of god has pushed us to this point, let us begin a new chapter. There is no point in looking back.

It is indeed a sad day when one has to express happiness at the demise of a corrupt but at least in appearance a democratic order. Many of us were jubilant in 1988 when democracy finally made a comeback. There was so much hope, so many expectations and a deep abiding optimism about the future of the country. In 1990, I quit the civil service (at that time I was joint secretary in the prime minister's secretariat) to join Benazir's crusade for democracy and people's welfare. How those dreams were dashed.

Nawaz was always corrupt and people were under no illusion about it but we hoped and prayed the Benazir would be different. This was not to be. In a strange quirk of fate, Nawaz Sharif had become a role model for most politicians. If he can amass money and thrive in politics, so ran the argument, others can too. In fact it had become a canon of faith for most politicians that if you have enough money, you can be anything or you can buy anything. I heard Asif Zardari publicly make this argument more than once. I know a number of senators of who bought their seats. So did some MNAs who had no previous political background but tons of money.

It was not just corruption, bad and reprehensible as it was. There was little commitment to democracy and no interest in governance. Corruption bankrupted us because huge, almost unbelievable sums of money were siphoned out of the country. Lack of commitment to democracy never allowed institutions to flourish. Poor governing methods took the sap out of an already crumbling state structure. This three pronged attack struck at the foundations of our state. A country that had so much promise was brought to a point where people started to talk of us as a failed state.

Nawaz was particularly ruthless in destroying institutions. To save their corrupt business practices and take dictatorial control of the country, the Sharifs specially targetted the judiciary. It was not just the physical attack on the Supreme Court, condemnable and unforgivable as it was. They did everything else to ensure a compliant judiciary. Family lawyers, personal friends, paid employees were inducted at every level. Less than cooperative judges were sidelined or sacked. Some were bribed or otherwise bought off. Through these tactics they were able to bring judiciary under their control. Benazir also got into a confrontation with the Supreme Court. At one time she seriously considered arresting the then chief justice of the Supreme Court, Sajjad Ali Shah. I did not hear this from anyone. I know.

Bureaucracy was politicised to an unbelievable extent. Officers came to be divided into camps. When Nawaz was in power a certain lot came on top and Benazir had her favourites. Junior officers like Rana Maqbool superseded hundreds to become IG Sindh. Benazir appointed her pilot as head of the KMC and her childhood friend as a federal secretary. A tottering state structure having serious problems as it is, almost seized to function. Those who resisted were taught a lesson. For the last three years now, some of the best officers in our service have been OSDs, meaning no job. Some others have been hounded out of service. This is how our leaders dealt with a premier institution of the state.

I am not sorry at the suspension of this democracy because this was no democracy. It was personal rule masquerading as democracy. It was also corrupt and incompetent. Above all the system was allowing the country to slide downhill at an alarming rate. The sounds emanating from the West are of no consequence to me. They do not know what we were going through. They were only satisfied that on paper we seemed to have everything that looked democratic.

The only thing positive that we had and which I hope the new government would also allow to function freely is the press. Nawaz made a serious attempt to browbeat the papers and to intimidate editors and journalists. Benazir to a lesser extent did her bit. It is testimony to the courage of the press that it resisted all such efforts and fought back. This institution must be preserved.

There is a long road ahead. There would be difficulties and problems. There would be provocations and temptations. There would be people, who always surround the centres of power, pushing their agendas. But a steady course will have to be pursued. At times unpopular decisions would have to be made for the good of the country and the people would be unhappy. But as long as the vision is clear and the objectives well defined, we as a nation shall not fail. God be with us all.

---

* Courtesy : *The Pakistan Times,* October, 24,1999

20

Implementing an Inescapable Agenda

* *M.S. Qazi*

General Musharraf, the chief executive (CE) of Pakistan in his nation-wide address on October 17 explicitly spelled out a seven-point agenda. The agenda is out-come of army high command's collective thinking to tide over existing national crises in a timeless frame to achieve tangible political, social and economic results to the satisfaction of people who because of development of events have been left in a lurch to look up to the army.

National agenda is public property and reflects people's latent aspirations to a large extent. Measures for its implementation are being eagerly awaited and many expectations are hinged on it. The raison d'etre of legitimation of constitutionally controversial military coup, apart from public antipathy to Nawaz Sharif's poor governance, his clash with state institutions and desire to concentrate power in his hands, lies in fulfilling public expectations. The CE has an uphill task to accomplish some of the public expectations.

The CE during the address allayed many fears, the most conspicuous among them being that Pakistan will be ruled under martial law. Instead, there is military rule sans martial law. The military rule is to be operated by a setup which will be 'primarily civilian.' National Security Council (NSC) which is likely to be heavily loaded with civilian technocrats will be the fulcrum of country's political power. It will be headed by the CE while CNS and CAS will be its two other members in uniform. The cabinet of ministers and thinktank body will work directly under the NSC. The new political setup is yet to take a concrete shape and work on sound footing. The outcome of functioning of new political setup in terms of delivering concrete results to the people within the parameters of national agenda is likely to be judged critically during next few months and could set critical pace for further legitimisation or otherwise of new political setup by the public.

Acquisition of power by the army has also gained legitimacy at the national level because she assumed political power as a counter-measure to the controversial sacking of the COAS (who was abroad) by the deposed PM in exercise of power vested in him by the Constitution. Nawaz Sharif's step did not enjoy the support of the army high command which was essentially required to legitimise the action taken under the Constitution. The welcome extended to the army by general public over assumption of political power further legitimised counter military coup. The question is: For how long the aura of legitimacy will last? Will it be for a few months or a few years from now?

Much will depend on the measures which through new political setup will be implemented and the results which would follow. Pakistan, unfortunately, is not new to military rule with martial law. The new experiment—military rule sans martial law—is being done for a variety reasons. Firstly, military rule for longer duration is unlikely to enjoy legitimacy and support in existing international environment dominated by the US and western countries. They are keen to see developing countries growing along with national democratic institutions. They have consciously made a break with their past tradition of Cold War era of supporting military dictators. It then suited them most. Now they have serious reservations and some of them have expressed their concern against the military rule in Pakistan.

Secondly, the three martial laws in 1958, 1969 and 1977 did not deliver the results promised by the military leaders. Ayub's martial law followed by his civilian rule weakened the federation of Pakistan to a state of terminal collapse. Yahya Khan's simply ensured terminal collapse of federation of Pakistan because of illconceived use of state power against the people of Pakistan. Zia's martial law divided the society into sectarian and ethnic divide whose reverberations and consequences are still being experienced.

The army has been conscious of these historical realities. Since 1988 when the democratic institutions started functioning in the country, she has been arbiter of power during four rounds of national crisis but did not opt to take over the reigns of power. Last year, then COAS supported deposed PM in his clash wth the CJ who was supported by then president and wanted to try the deposed PM on charges of corruption.

The former COAS also made a rather embarrassing exit when his perceptions to run the state affairs were at variance with the perceptions of deposed PM and he made them public during his address at the Naval War College. It is publicly known that the army despite COAS's differences with the deposed PM for a variety of reasons had ruled out any "extra-constitutional" measures to overthrow the government of deposed PM wrongly echoed by Washington, till he himself attempted through a very irrational step to remove the COAS and tried to hand over the command of the army to a loyalist general with very intriguing intentions. Notwithstanding the constitutional blanket power that the deposed PM enjoyed, his power game would have serious implications for the country.

The army is in commanding position with great responsibilities on her shoulders. Will she deliver the results this time as promised by the CE? One has to appreciate three vital points in this regard. Firstly, the aura of legitimacy which military rule enjoys presently will be comparatively shortlived because the army has assumed power in a power struggle against an established civilian government headed by a powercrazy PM and not because of open rejection of civilian government by the people as it had happened in 1969 and 1977.

Secondly, during Nawaz Sharif's rule (and earlier also) the public has seen facade of democracy in action wherein clash between PM and president took place with the exit of latter, clash between PM and judiciary (the CJ) also took place with humiliating exit of the latter and the federal government made excessive use of state power and extra constitutional means against real political forces in the province of Sindh to keep the latter out of corridors of power. Finally, they have seen the PM and COAS struggling against each other—the latter prevailing upon the former on October 12.

These clashes and their result have consequently led to the failure of state institutions rather than failure of a PM, All this also reflected a broader failure among various centres of power who could not agree to make the Constitution work. This failure of institutions was the deep rooted cause of breaking up of federation of Pakistan in 1971. Since then the malice in one form or the other has continuously persisted.

How will new political setup address the issue of strengthening the federation? The outline of new political setup so far made public is ill-equipped to handle such a sensitive and huge national task. So is the army. The federation can be strengthened only by the political parties and direct participation of people in the political process. It has been amply demonstrated by the failure of retrogressive measures adopted by Ayub Khan and Zia for smooth functioning of the federation sans people's participation in dubious political processes engineered by them. Any deviation from the universally accepted instruments of genuine democratic setup, power to people's representative who have genuine desire to work for the people and people's direct participation in their own affairs, would be quite dangerously counter-productive for the country.

Out of seven points, the two points—revival of economy and restoring investors' confidence and ensuring swift and across the board accountability—should be targeted by the new setup on priority basis. It would be a tremendous achievement if substantial gains are made on these items. The accountability process has to be apolitical, transparent and across-the-board to gain credibility at national and international levels. Substantial results on the two points can be achieved with 18 to 24 months. Remaining five points of CE's agenda are laudable but cannot make headway without direct public participation through political parties. For the a larger timeframe and active participation of those who wield political power are essential. This is beyond the 'limited' mandate, which the army has been tacitly given by the people.

The seven-point agenda is not escapable for the survival of the country and for making progress in all facets of national life. The army at this crucial juncture could make a very positive contribution by seeking public vote to amend the Constitution only to strengthen the federation and to make Constitution workable but not prolong her stay in power. The amendments should envisage system of checks and balances which has been fiddled by PPP and PML governments during their tenures after implementation of the Constitution in 1971.

All eyes are set on the army. It is destined to play a crucial role to revitalise economy, hold accountable corrupt elements irrespctive to which segment to society from they belong and finally adopt measures which should strengthen the federation and make Constitution and democratic institutions functional. Substantial gains can be made in all these spheres within 18 to 24 months in case the army high command makes conscious efforts and establishes a direct relationship between a timeframe and the goal to be achieved. Any aspirations going beyond a timeframe of 18 to 24 months would negate the legitimacy which presently military leaders enjoy and people's trust which they have reposed in them. The longer their stay in power more wary will be the people as our past history clearly demonstrates.

Courtesy : *The Frontier Post (Pakistan)*, October 25, 1999.

21

Sensing the Future Course

* *Shireen M. Mazari*

General Pervaiz Musharraf's address to the nation on October 17 was significant not only in what it said, but also in what it left unsaid. By examining both these aspects, one can begin to have a sense of the direction in which the country is going to be led. The overriding principle that seemed to underline the general's speech was a clear-cut commitment to domestic priorities and a national approach to external policy. So, while the general reasserted Pakistan's commitment to its allies and important global powers like the US, it was made equally clear that Pakistan is not going to play to the tune of these powers.

For instance, no mention was made of any envisaged time span for the restoration of "true democracy" that the general committed to in principle. This omission was all the more stark because in their usual cacophony of ignorance the major powers have been clamouring for "restoration of democracy" as soon as possible—as if the sole purpose behind the military takeover was the removal of the Sharif government and now that had been achieved the decaying system should be left to continue functioning as it had been. After all, weak national institutions and a corrupt system are so much easier for external interests to infiltrate. General Musharraf has sent a clear signal to these external forces that until the country's internal institutions and domestic polity are not stabilised, there can be no question of a "restoration of democracy". From the address it also appears that there may well be a new democratic system in the offing—instead of the quasi-functional parliamentary system that has been decimated by the political elite.

The whole tenor of the general's address was a message to the external powers and forces that at present, at least, Pakistan's decision-makers are going to do what is important within the national context. That is why, while discussing the fragile state of the economy, the general made no mention of the IMF and other international financial institutions that have revealed their political nature in the manner in which they have linked future disbursements to the "return of democracy". But then they also know that they have more room to dictate and destroy when corrupt "democratic" governments are in place. Equally interesting was the lack of a need to seek these institutions as scapegoats for the country's ills. Instead, the general clearly admitted that the country had hit rockbottom due to its own leader's shenanigans. This is how it should be—whatever the interventions and interferences of international institutions, it is the national leadership that allows them that privilege.

In the face of no timetable for the revival of any electoral system, the general's commitment to basic rights and especially freedom of the media can be of some comfort for the nation. But so much depends on how things operationalise from now on. The romance between the military and the people may flourish if the latter feel they can breathe freely and easily and not have their basic human rights trampled on. Otherwise the romance will be replaced by increasing acrimony and dissent. For the political elite, there is going to be an indefinite period in which they should do serious soul-searching on their role within the national polity. Ms. Bhutto, at least, should educate herself on some basics. For instance, she would do well to find out what a "civil war" is! And Mr. Sharif and his co-conspirators may well examine the sheer horrendousness of their decision to risk the lives of so many innocent people simply to satisfy their urge for total control. The whole plane episode will be a traumatic reminder of how little value the ruling elite placed on human life.

From the national perspective, the most welcome part of the address was the clear-cut condemnation of the exploitation of religion. Together with the reassurance given to the minorities, this should begin to put Pakistan back on the path envisaged by Jinnah. One hopes that this will be followed by action on the ground against sectarian and obscurantist groups/parties.

On foreign and security policies, while the general maintained that there would be no change, his focus on Kashmir and the Muslim world were critical. For too long, governments in Pakistan have said one thing and done another on Kashmir. A strong, unambivalent political commitment and support for the Kashmiri mujahideen was the need of the hour. Let us hope that we will now have a proactive and unapologetic policy on Kashmir.

The statement that the Muslim world will be central to Pakistan's foreign relations hopefully will be followed up by some concrete moves like evolving a 'Community of Power' with some Muslim states of the region. Also, the critical OIC secretary-general's elections make it imperative for Pakistan to play a highly proactive role within the OIC.

The fact that the general did not waste too much time on the nuclear issue—focusing only on the need to stabilise the nuclear deterrence mutually with India—shows that as far as Pakistan is concerned, the nuclear factor is a reality that the world must accept since it is not going to alter. And, now that the US Senate has made the CTBT practically redundant, the general sensibly did not waste time on this issue. Perhaps he could have assured the international community by committing to abide by the MTCR guidelines. Meanwhile, there are rumours of US nuclear inspectors having been in Pakistan very recently and one hopes that any suspected compromises on the country's nuclear programme will be revealed to the nation.

On Afghanistan, General Musharraf's support for a "broad-based government" does signal at least a shift in nuance in Pakistan's Afghan policy. Linked with the issue of exploitation of religion, the free run given to the Taliban should end and a more pragmatic policy should be operationalised soon.

Of course, at the end of the day, no foreign policy can be effective unless those in charge of operationalising it are clear-cut in their approch. Here, the Foreign Office needs to be reformed appropriately so that a less western-oriented mindset evolves. Fear of what the US may or may not do needs to be eliminated from the corridors of power.

Overall, the address, with its matter-of-fact tone and content, with no grandiose chest-beating was the need of the hour. For once all blame for our ills was also placed squarely on ourselves and not on external forces. Now, the present decision-makers must also reject external diktat. The idea that the US ambassador intended to hold a press conference after the chief executive's address smacks of smug viceregal pretensions. It would be appropriate to put such a diplomat in his place. This would send the correct message to the international community that while Pakistan may be in dire straits, it is not, about to kow-tow to foreign powers.

As for the Commonwealth seeking to suspend Pakistan's membership, it is too bad that General Musharraf did not temporarily take Pakistan out of the Commonwealth himself. But at the end of the day, foreign investment by individual Commonwealth countries in not dependent on membership to that organisation so the loss in real terms is not critical.

Three objections to the address need to be highlighted. One, that it was addressed to "countrymen" only. Two, following from that, it was unfortunate that while minorities were reassured, women, who have been mistreated by successive regimes, were not single out for a similar reassurance of their basic human rights. While these were in all probability an oversight of the military mind, it would serve the general well to be aware of these points for the future.

A third objection—or one can see it as a disappointment—is on the retention of Mr. Tarar as the country's president. Tarar's links to obscurantist groups, his protection of madaris after coming to power and his overall professional track record is a constant reminder of all that has been wrong with the democratic setups of Pakistan. But perhaps we need to constantly be faced with such a reminder.

Be that as it may, General Musharraf has made a realistic start to governance — a start devoid of grandstanding and one which acknowledges the severe national shortcomings exposed by our ruling elite for over five decades. If such a hardnosed confrontation of reality continues to counter the headiness of power, then perhaps this nation may enter the new millennium on an even keel.

---

* Courtesy: *The Pakistan Times,* October, 22, 1999

22

The Takeover and Thereafter

* *Qudssia Akhlaque*

If the October 12 army take-over was demise of democracy, the popular reactions to it clearly suggested it was a happy one. The jubilationstemmed from the promise that this demise would give birth to social justice and orderly life for the people of Pakistan. There are signs showing already that Pakistan's heavy majority is justified in sharing this optimism this time round.

The sense of relief across the country at the dismissal of an elected civilian leader through a bloodless coup by men in khaki is unprecedented. The ensuing popular reaction goes only to show that people never had anyfaith in the institutions that make democracy work in a system. People seemwilling to trust the credibility of the Army as a doer rather than a quickfix set-up that would kick start the institutions of the state and stage an exit in 90 days.

General Musharraf came up to these expectations when he promised results rather than elections. Lack of timeframe only added to the optimism and General Musharraf's credibility. The General's announcement of his agenda five days after 'moving in' was received with consensus opinion that this is no 90-day programme and that the present administration could be fairly regarded as Pakistan's last hope. The optimism is not even guarded and still seems justified.

Three days after the announcement of a four-week ultimatum to the loandefaulters responsible for the mega robbery of Rs. 225 billion belonging to banks and financial institutions, a company belonging to Nawaz Sharif's main henchman Saifur Rahman stood in the Court offering to repay its loanover-dues of Rs. 1.1 billion. The prospect of across the board-accountability is already showing results.

The credit for the widely welcomed coup goes to Sharif's self-defeating policies and actions. It demonstrates how rapidly a government with even a historic massive mandate can become unpopular if it fails to deliver. A government that deviates from the path of democracy or distorts it. That abuses its mandate to bypass and violate all democratic norms for its ownself preservation. For democrats Nawaj's rule should be a lesson in what democracy should not be. And those now at the helm of affairs should beware of those pitfalls. Sharif's unceremonious ouster should serve as a constant reminder to those in charge that even the most popular regimes can lose support faster than they gain it if they falter and blunder.

The new self-appointed chief executive carries the heavy burden of cleaning up the monumental mess created by successive democratic governments. He has to move decisively but with care and caution to ensure that his regime does not become part of this mess. Gen. Musharraf has set before him admirable objectives of putting the house in order but achieving these objectives may take a long time. In that case people are bound to lose their patience, as they did in case of Nawaz Sharif. The speed with which he executes his seven-point agenda is equally important, if not more. It takes very little for the goodwill to erode. One wrong move by him or his appointees and supporters of the coup makers can become their biggest critics too. Euphoria can soon turn into cynicism. After all even the best intentioned agenda if badly executed can prove to be disastrous.

One knows that Gen. Musharraf carries no Allahdin's lamp but people have very high expectations of him. His declaration that "this is not a martial law" has further raised these expectations. He has to therefore be watchful that he or his men do not resort to any actions that are a reminder of the much condemned martial law days. We can ill afford that the image of the army, to quote Gen. Musharraf "the last viable institution in the country" be tarnished.

While the General has been encouraged by the support he has received from the people he must bear in his mind that the same support can dwindle if he does not deliver fast. There is no point in wasting time condemning the previous administration because Nawaz Sharif has already paid dearly for his misdeed. We have to look ahead and focus on what needs to be done and how it ought to be done.

Gen. Musharraf's statement that "we will not stay in charge any longer than is required," has been generally welcomed but it has also raised questions. The necessary timeframe could mean years if he is looking at completion of his heavy agenda. But perhaps the General is playing it safe, having before him the example of Gen. Zia-ul-Haq who announced elections in 90 days but continued to rule for eleven years. By giving a specific timeframe Gen. Musharraf realised he would have run the risk of going back on his word and faced the credibility issue in case of compulsions to stay on longer. Also, by not giving a timeframe he made it clear that he means business and would not be bogged down by any deadline. That he will go ahead with his reformist agenda and that only once things are in place for "real democracy" would he make an exit. But even in the absence of a timetable any attempt to "overstay" can create problems for him.

Perhaps it would be in best interest of the country if the present regime focuses on across the board accountability, recovery of money from loan and tax defaulters, and electoral reforms that facilitate entry of more competent, honest and sincere people into the political arena. Equally important is to strengthen judiciary and devise a mechanism of checks and balances that can be sustained and not challenged by any subsequent government in Islamabad.

Gen. Musharraf in his address to the nation said: "our actions will speak louder than words" and so they must indeed. People are fed up of endless rhetoric. Don't say it, do it, is the plea of millions of Pakistanis who want to see their country prosper and progress. They want promises backed by performance, results not rhetoric. Most of all they want relief not redundancy.

Mindful of such concerns, the new administration under General Musharraf is attacking core economic issues of loan and tax defaults by the industrial and business elite. These are sigs of possible success already. The General-turned-chief executive could find himself perfectly poised to steer reform if he can announce substantial progress on this front at the end of four weeks on November 16.

---

* Courtesy : *The Pakistan Times,* November 1, 1999

23

Corruption Public Enemy Number One

* *Kalim Dil Khan*

Very shortly, as a nation we shall be stepping into the new millennium. At this particular juncture every nation takes a cool stock of its past performance and thereby resolves to enter the new millennium with an indomitable vigour and renewed spirit. In juxtaposition to the international trend, we are caught in a state of inertia. Leave aside entering the new millennium with a new furor, we are standing at the crossroads of history, totally perplexed and haggard with a weighty milestone of corruption around our neck and the restrictive fetters of foreign debt in our feet.

Pakistan, today, is confronted with gigantic problems. They are vast and varied in nature. Out of them five major problems i.e. corruption, poverty, population growth, illiteracy, and deteriorating law and order situation have plagued Pakistan ever since its inception. The cumulative effect of them all has generated a total economic chaos. The politicians with all their cognitive powers and the military rules with all their might, taking turns alternatively, have not been able to find an enduring solution to these nagging problems for the last 52 years. Whenever there is a political change, the new leadership promises us a rose garden with a lot of sunshine, but very often, after a brief breathing interval, the same dark clouds of despair again haunt us. All the new promises made by every new leadership turns out to be the same old dross. Hence, the fate of the common man has remained unchanged, he is still wallowing in the quagmire of poverty, while the oligarchs who pervaded through our politics have piled up stacks of hay while the sun was shining on them.

The five intractable socio-economic problems that haunt Pakistan are fundamentally intertwined. Prudence requires that they should be discussed collectively, but that may fudge the core issue of corruption. The issue at hand is too gigantic to be obscured by bracketing it with the rest of the socio-economic problems. It has brought us the notoriety of being number two on the list of the corrupt nations, on the domestic front it has turned out to be as our public enemy No. 1.

Although nowadays, the most talked-about malaise of Pakistan is the crumbling economy, in reality that too is a corollary of corruption. The economic cost of corruption is horrendours. It not only impedes our economic growth, it also scares away foreign and domestic investment. It accelerates human poverty, threateners the legitimacy of the state and saps human development. Moreover, the corrupt money never stays within the country to enhance its investment and production. It gets siphoned out and takes abode in foreign banks. Besides its economic cost, its cancerous tentacles have already sunk deep roots in our social and political milieu.

In order to quantify the problem and to trace its roots, we have to probe into the post-independence period. We need to find answers to some unanswered questions such as: why our independence could not become the instrument of our progress and happiness? Why opportunism prevails in our policies? Why is there so much of distrust for politicians and public office-holders? Pakistan was created to protect the Muslims of the sub-continent from the opportunistic politics of Hindu majority and to accord an opportunity to the Muslim minority to galvanise their lives in accordance with the teachings of Islam.

The Quaid-e-Azam believed in an end to discrimination, domination and deprivation. It was the raison d'etre of his political struggle. In order to achieve it, he aimed first at gaining political freedom, while his ultimate objective was to ensure economic freedom. Unfortunately his bad health and untimely death prevented him from accomplishing his agenda. Political freedom is a 'tool', on acquisition, it is invariably used to achieve economic freedom. Unless a nation has attained the latter, it cannot ensure socio-economic justice to its people, nor can independence become the instrument of progress and happiness for that nation.

Throughout the struggle for independence, our immediate desire was to gain political freedom, under no circumstance was it our ultimate desire. More often, during such protracted struggle the activists get focus on their immediate desire, it is being desired so vehemently that on fulfilment of it, in total frenzy of happiness, they lose sight of their ultimate desire. Precisely that has happened to the common man in the post-independence scenario. The gullible masses, in the frenzy of jubilation, lost sight of their ultimate desire. The opportunists took advantage of this setback; they immediately seized the 'tool' i.e. the political power that was the net outcome of the political freedom. Instead of sharing the 'tool' with all for the collective good of all, they monopolised it and started utilising it exclusively for self-aggrandisement, thus the trend was set for opportunistic politics.

That trend continues even today in a much more aggravated form. There is a large breed of politicians who take huge loans from the state exchequer, utilising half of it for their over-invoiced business venture and the remaining half on their political campaigns. And in one go they become parliamentarians-cum-industrialists at the cost of tax-payers' money. Afterwards by using their political clout, the loans are eventually written off or rescheduled to their utmost convenience. This is the recipe in vogue for success in politics. Such tactics have brought infamy to our democracy. Our democracy is dubbed as wayward because it has always shielded such opportunistic politicians and has helped them in perpetuating the *incumbency lock* that exists in our politics.

The second tragedy of our politics has been to keep the common man out of the 'system'. At no level has he been associated with decision-making, as such he has become politically atrophied by sheer disuse. His natural instinct for constructiveness remained dormant. On the contrary, the ruling elite had been enjoying undiluted power having no fear, whatsoever, from the politically atrophied masses. As a result their impulse for naked power was growing from strength to strength. When the impulse gets stronger its first casualty is the foresight. Since they are inversely proportional to each other, one negates the other. If the foresight is strong it may falsify the impulse, but if the impulse is robust it will consume the foresight and disagreeble results will ensue. Since the 1950s due to the feeble foresight of our leaders the ship of our democracy is adrift.

The Siamese Twins of opportunism and corruption that entered our body politics in the 1950s gradually proliferated into almost all the institutions and started gnawing at the very roots of our state. A newly formed state is comparable to a newly born infant—an organic body especially vulnerable to and in need of protection from mortal viruses that can wreak havoc with both its physiological and psychological development. Psychology teaches us that the suppression of various natural instincts of a person will ensue different mental disorders, such a person may remain warped. His abilities are sapped by the psychological disorder and ultimately that individual may become a pervert. A newly born state too, like an individual, becomes a prey to numerous ills when its natural instincts are disregarded, or when its wild impulses are not pruned prudently.

Pathology teaches us how HIV consumes the immune system of an individual. A state too, just like an individual, has its own immune system, i.e. an independent judiciary, independent media and honest law-enforcing agencies constitute the immune system of a state. Two-thirds of our state's immune system is already dibilitated by the deadly virus of corruption. If curative steps are not taken in time our state is bound to slip deeper into the deadly syndrome of acquired immune deficiency. The new leadership has to show exceptional courage, patience and perseverance to steer the ship of the state away from the turbulent water, skilfully avoiding the rock of Scylla and the whirlpool of Charybdis. If the new leadership sincerely sets its priorities right sooner than later, the atrophied common man will be inspired and his weariness and discouragement will be turned into energy and ardour.

---

* Courtesy : *The Frontier Post (Pakistan)*, November 3, 1999.

24

New Tasks Ahead

* *Asad Rahman*

Nearly three weeks have passed since the government of Nawaz Sharif was sent home in a dramatic manner. The general public breathed a sigh of relief. Expectations of the people soured with the new military regime's agenda of accountability, economic revival, cleaning up of the political morass and laying the foundations of true democracy. The jubilation seen immediately after the events of October 12 soon descended into a pregnant wait-and-see mode. Slowly but surely this is turning into disappointment and visible unease creeping into the people's minds.

The appointments made to the NSC and of some ministers have to a great extent been questionable, to say the least. Apart from one governor, Amirul Mulk Mengal in Balochistan, the other three have not inspired much confidence. In an effort to appease international opposition to the coup (or counter-coup, as Gen. Pervaiz Musharraf described it), President Rafiq Tarar has been asked to remain in office while the Supreme Court has been asked to support the noble goals of the new regime.

The continuation of the president in office may be politically expedient for the new regime but it has left a bitter taste in the mouth of most political observers. Many of the actions of the present incumbent prior to his election to his office were suspicious at the time of commission. It is alleged that he played a central role in the unceremonious removal of the then chief Justice Sajjad Ali Shah, who was hearing a contempt case agaisst Nawaz Sharif. This action also forced the then president, Farooq Leghari, to resign thus paving the way for his own election. Mr. Tarar, by association, also contributed to the attack on the Supreme Court in the same case. His undying and longstanding loyalty to the Sharif family in well known. He had unquestioningly implemented and supported all the undemocratic and autocratic policies of Nawaz. In this background keeping him on, even if for ceremonial purposes, raises questions that are leading to a perception that some incomprehensible compromises are in the offing.

Corruption has permeated all sections of our society, be it politicians, bureaucrats, or some members of the judiciary. The recent forced retirement, suspension and ouster of judicial officers in the lower ranks are a confirmation of the corruption in the judiciary. I do not agree with the language used by my erstwhile colleague Ardeshir Cowasjee, but the general drift of what he said is the common perception regarding the judiciary. The contempt case against his utterances further brings into question the judgement in the Supreme Court storming case by PML stalwarts, where some people were charged but got away scot-free, ostensibly for lack of evidence and witnesses.

Critics of the judiciary have been emboldened by the actions, statements and politically motivated judgements of some of the judges themselves and thus the more open nature of the criticism. The atmosphere of animosity in the court, reported in the Cowasjee case itself, has raised questions on its impartiality and bias. A fire burns where there is smoke and if there is so much of criticism then there has to be at least a grain of truth in it. I believe that the judiciary must command respect instead of demanding it.

I have grown up in a judge's home and met many judges of impeccable character and international stature against whom no one could ever pass an adverse remark such as are being espoused at this time in our history. Their judgements, social behaviour and court etiquette are stil! remembered and quoted with fond and proud feelings.

The socio-political and economic quagmire that we find ourselves in has been analysed and written about ad finitum. We seem to know where we have gone wrong but solutions have never been forthcoming. Radical surgery is the need of the hour and although the new regime seems to have the right agenda, it is moving too slowly and with some uncertainty. This slow pace, although understandable, could contribute to disillusionment very quickly and may as well erode people's support for this government. Although there are no quick-fix solutions to the enormous problems faced by the nation, there are some that need to be instituted on a war-footing. The much flaunted across-the-board accountability process must be speeded up. Those that have been arrested on corruption, anti-state charges must be brought to book immediately and their lists published. Special courts will have to be established to try these enemies of the people. The present courts have been politicised to too great an extent to meet this challenge.

On the economic front, instead of loan defaulters, the need is to concentrate on getting back the ill-gotten wealth stashed away in foreign safe havens by politicians, bureaucrats, and industrialists to Pakistan. Eight out of ten defaulters are genuine defaulters who suffered losses and closure of businesses due to government's erratic policies, mismanagement or other factors. No doubt they too must be vigorously pursued, but one feels that the reported US $80 to $100 billion transferred abroad by our corrupt officials is the real answer to Pakistan's economic woes. Even if 50 per cent of this amount comes back into the national exchequer, it would help us get out of the exploitative and dictatorial clutches of the IMF and World Bank.

If Pakistan is to stand on its own two feet and avoid all the international pressures over Kashmir, our nuclear programme, system of governance and economic policies, then we have to get rid of the huge foreign debt first and foremost. This is the best opportunity available to the government of the day to get this wealth back. I believe any and all means of persuasion must be applied to the looters of this wealth to make them transfer these funds to Pakistan. To do this one of the first steps to undertake would be to defreeze the foreign currency accounts thereby giving an incentive to the business and industrial houses to transfer their money back and ban residents of Pakistan from holding accounts abroad.

Along with this reduce the number (reportedly about 65) of direct and indirect taxes that citizens have to pay to a minimum. Reduce the number of departments that an industrialist has to pay graft to from some 22 to a maximum of five. These measures will encourage taxpayers and widen the tax net.

One of the factors why citizens are reluctant to pay taxes is the misuse of the public money by governments. The Baitul Mal and collection of zakat is a prime example of the misuse of people's funds. Wealth tax is another such tax that needs to be reviewed and possibly withdrawn. In fact all taxes on savings must be withdrawn to encourage savings and accumulation of wealth for investment in the country thereby creating jobs and reducing unemployment. Tax on education must also be withdrawn to develop our human resources. The tax regime needs rationalisation and simplification to significantly expand the number of tax-paying citizens from just about a million or two out of 130 million.

The present regime must create a permanent, independent, impartial accountability process and establish an independent, impartial judiciary and Election Commission. Use the time required to establish these institutions wisely and with foresight. While persuading the looters to bring back their ill-gotten wealth, compile new voters' lists and issue computerised national identity cards. Stabilise the economy by giving incentives to business and industrial houses to start investment in country and establish a price and wage commission to avoid unjustified profits and exploitation. These measures must be the priority while obviously taking other radical measures to pull Pakistan out of its political and economic mess. Somehow with the appointments made so far the government have not generated the confidence needed to assure the people that the appointed people can fulfill the onerous tasks ahead. Let us hope that the next batch of appointments is better and more competent to deliver.

---

* Courtesy : *The Pakistan Times,* November 6, 1999

25

Options Before the New Set-Up

* *ABMS Zahur*

Ever since the promulgation of the Constitution of 14 August 1973 it was amended 14 times mainly to increase the power of the prime minister. During the last 26 years (1973-99) all the three prime ministers (ZA Bhutto, Benazir Bhutto and Mian Nawaz Sharif) were afraid of the army because democracy in real sense could never grow in Pakistan nor any of the prime ministers was interested in strengthening its democratic base. ZA Bhutto was interested in increasing his power and perpetuating his rule, Benazir was interested in personal gains at the cost of the country and Nawaz Sharif was not satisfied with only that he wanted to be a king of that country. Strictly speaking, democracy never existed in Pakistan. Thus ousting of Nawaz Sharif may not be seen as a big blow to democratic base of the country. In fact Sharif's rule has been a tyranny under the facade of democracy.

The people voted Sharif overwhelmingly with the hope that he would provide them with better governance, improve the economy and establish the rule of law. Instead, he gave them worst form of cronyism and greed for power. In short, he took the following steps to satisfy his lust:

Strangulation of parliament through the fourteenth amendment;

Removal of President Leghari;
Removal of the chief justice.

Persecution of the opposition through a discriminatory process of *ehtesab*;

Meddling in the affairs of the armed forces and removal of naval and army chiefs.

Virtually transforming the federal structure of government into a unitary form by usurpation of provincial autonomy.

Introduction of Shariat bill (could not, howerver, be passed due to lack of obtaining two thirds majority vote in the senate). He messed up the economy of Pakistan. His economic packages for revival of the economy were neither well conceived nor properly executed. There was enormous increase in tax evasion, and reduction in tax collection. Defaulted loans increased significantly. The loss of public sector enterprises rose to over Rs. 150 billion a year. Mishandling of foreign investors, freezing foreign currency accounts and arbitrary changes in economic policies led to continual erosion in investors' confidence.

In short, Pakistan is practically insolvent and heavily dependent on the international donor agencies such as the IMF, World Bank and Asian Development Bank and the grace and sympathy of G-7 countries. Her foreign exchange reserve is less than up $1.5 billion, foreign debt burden is US$33 billion, loan-defaulters' outstanding loan is $3.92 billion according to some estimate US$ 5 billion). Her risk rating is so low that she cannot borrow from commercial banks. Her rescheduling arrangement has not yet been successful because of IMF's postponement of ESAF programme.

Pakistan has started losing its comparative advantage even in its traditionally strong sectors. Agriculture has also lost its buoyancy because of continuous rise in the prices of inputs, falling yield and falling prices of agricultural products. Now to save this sad and sick nation Gen. Musharraf has mainly the following aims and objectives:

Rebuilding national confidence and morale;

Strengthening the federation;

Reviving the economy and restoring investors' confidence; and

Ensuring law and order.

So far he has appointed four provincial governors. Three of them are retired armed forces' personnel and the fourth is a retired provincial high court judge. In a meeting held on 21 October 1999 (chaired by him) he told that he would take strict measures against loan defaulters, tax evadors and all others responsible for the prevailing economic crisis.

Making such promises may not be difficult but their fulfilment depends on full cooperation of the people. It may be possible to straighten up the problems of tax evasion, collection of revenues and loan default within a couple of years but a long-term risky exercise will be necessary for return of ill-gotten wealth locally and from abroad because this exercise will affect the politicians, bureaucrats and even some uniformed personnel (serving and retired), businessmen and industrialists who are very powerful because of their wealth and connections. After all, life's way is king's way and money rules there. Even if laws are enacted for the recovery off ill-gotten wealth their execution may not be at all easy.

Without gearing up of economic performance no sustainable development is possible. For development, human ingenuity and release of human potential are needed. This is not possible in a military rule. The history of Pakistan itself proves that sustainable development is difficult under military rule. Despite the 26 years of so-called efficient governance (during army rules) the country is politically and economically underdeveloped. We see absolutely no reason as to why it would be otherwise this time. Furthermore, this time Pakistan is facing the threats of economic sanctions from the United States, European Community and Japan. Her membership of Commonwealth has been suspended.

The SAARC nations are worried as to what is to be done to Pakistan. US has already cut off economic and military aid. However, US is not "walking away" from Pakistan. Though US has made it clear that longterm military control is not acceptable and democracy must be restored.

Under the circumstances the only option appears to be open to Gen. Musharraf is to continue his rule for not more than six months. He may give a framework of governance acceptable to the Supreme Court of Pakistan and the donor agencies and G-7 nations. A strategic economic programme with clear objective may be prepared. He may start its implementation leaving its continuity to the elected governments. Apparently, the success of Musharraf depends on the honesty, objectivity, sincerity of purpose and professional competence of the people associated in formulating and implementing the policies, mere sincere and competent leadership with foresight and acumen may not be enough. He needs an excellent team to accomplish the defined objectives.

It all depends on how far he will be able to form such a team. And while time is running out he will have to move fast. Any delay may make the whole exercise as the tantrum of a dismissed general.

---

* Courtesy : *The Frontier Post, (Pakistan),* November 6, 1999

26

The General Speaks

** Farrukh Saleem*

The two aspects of General Musharraf's speech on October 17 that very few missed were his determination to put Pakistan back on the right track and, two, the army's willingness to take the responsibility of steering the country into the right direction. The other two issues on which the jury shall remain out for a while are, one, the army's institutional capability to actually accomplish the goals that it has set for itself and the general's ability to lead a major peace-time civilian effort which he hasn't been trained for.

The army's agenda as set by the general's speech broadly falls into political goals, economic objectives and our foreign policy strategy. Under political goals, the chief executive has committed to stay for no longer than it would be absolutely necessary. Under the new setup the armed forces intend to "strengthen the federation" and "remove inter-provincial disharmony."

International reaction on this count is well represented by James Rubin of the US Department of State. The spokesman said that the "United States is pleased to hear that the new military regime in Pakistan intends to restore democracy and constitutional rule" but "we are disappointed that General Pervaiz Musharraf did not offer a clear timetable". On the domestic front, most

Pakistanis have had enough of democracy and their current emphasis is on some real food on the table rather than a democratic facade. A more specific timetable for a future election would have silenced critics outside of Pakistan, but if the chief executive can actually manage to deliver, a majority of Pakistanis shall continue to cherish a government run by a military-technocratic setup led by the National Security Council (NSC).

Under economic objectives, the chief executive's priority lies in the revival of the economy and the restoration of "investor confidence". The two are surely interlinked. On the international front, resolution of the Hubco deal has become a test case of Pakistan's ability to attract foreign capital in the future. What has been lacking in the past is honesty while negotiating with international institutional investors. Tenaga Nasional Berhad, the huge Malaysian energy concern and the owner of Liberty Power, for instance, just recently accused that someone in the Nawaz government had asked for $10 million to make things easy for Liberty. Hopefully, the new government would introduce the element of honesty while negotiating with foreign institutional operators and eventually mend fences with them.

On the domestic front, its unfortunate but all that this country has is some 2,000 active business families. That's all we have as domestic investors. They are all interconnected either through corporate partnerships or through inter-marriages. A large number of them, either willingly or because of adverse business conditions, have been unable to pay back bank loans. The money has either been lost or has evaporated up in thin air never to come back. It the government now begins to harass this class of investors or starts throwing them behind bars the domestic business environment shall take another beating.

To be honest, recovery of defaulted loans is no more than a popular political slogan. It has no economic significance whatsoever. From a more theoretical standpoint, of the Rs. 300 billion in defaulted loans a good 50 per cent is accumulated interest. It shall be highly unreasonable to expect that people who have failed to pay the principal amount could be made to pay interest.

If the government did nothing else but devoted all its energies for the following 10 years on trying to recover loans gone sour, it may with a lot of luck collect some 25 per cent of the outstanding principal. What that means is some Rs. 40 billion and that equates to what the government spends in 20 days.

As far as politically directed loans are concerned, almost by definition, these loans would have little or no collateral. A more practical landmark in regards to accountability would have been to draw a firm line and make sure that no more politically directed loans are given out.

On the issue of public sector enterprises, trying to turn them around is not going to work. It hasn't worked anywhere else on the face of the planet neither does stand much chance in this country. Privatization, on the other hand, has been a proven success around the globe.

On the foreign policy front, a willingness to enter into a "result oriented" dialogue with India and a unilateral deescalation of troops along the international border were both strokes of ingenuity. A military government advising Afghanistan to have a representative government wasn't, however, that good of an idea. The stage is now set for UN-imposed sanctions on the Taliban regime and Pakistan, the lone supporter, would be hard pressed to implement them.

---

* Courtesy : *The Pakistan Times,* October, 22,1999

27

Tough Decisions Ahead

* *Mir Jamllur Rahman*

It was a ludicrous sight: The TV screen showing an army officer fastening the general's pips on the shoulder of Lt General Khwaja Ziauddin with the newscaster announcing his appointment as the new COAS in place of General Pervaiz Musharraf. A bureaucrat from the prime minister's office was watching the disgusting ceremony with a broad grin.

The army moved swiftly and decisively. Had it not done so, the army, as an institution, would have suffered an irreparable division endangering the security of the country. The army's response to this indignity cannot be faulted for it has saved the country from a big disaster. The legal minds could ensure the army's action for its constitutional deviation. However, the fact remains that the people have backed the action. All the opposition parties have expressed relief. Even some prominet PML legislators have welcomed the action. The newspaper comments have described the action as inevitable. The government of Nawaz Sharif had indeed become unpopular.

The heavily-mandated government had become unpopular because it had transgressed constitutional and legal boundaries. It was conducting the government business more dictatorially than a dictator would. It was getting increasingly unethical. The end of such a government, as our history has repeatedly shown has always been tragic.

The order to retire Gen Musharraf was not only unethical but also had an element of chicanery in it. Only two weeks ago Shahbaz Sharif and Chaudhry Nisar Ahmed had met Gen Musharraf to reassure him that the government has full confidence in him. The government demonstrated its unbounded confidence by confirming him as the chairman of the Joint Chiefs of Staff Committee. As the later events proved, it was a ploy though it rebounded on its perpetrators.

Now the army is in the saddle and Gen Musharraf is the chief executive (CE), which is a humanised substitute for chief martial law administrator. The constitution is in abeyance, which means that for all practical purposes the country is now under martial law, thanks to Nawaz Sharif and his gang of upstart colleagues. The overthrow of Nawaz Sharif was easy because despite the PTV propaganda he had become an immensely disliked head of government. The difficult task lies ahead, which the new chief executive would soon discover.

The international pressure on Gen Musharraf would be immense to restore democracy. He would be literally besieged to make the transitory period short. The international community would warn him of economic boycott if he did not renew the democratic process. However, Gen Musharraf would not be able to do so because of the countervailing domestic pressure. Almost every political leader has been crying hoarse for accountability first and democracy later. They have been demanding a two-year moratorium on democracy for the purpose of across-the-board accountability.

The chief executive may tread the accountability track for 20 years and yet it would remain an unfinished business. Some former government leaders could be barred from politics by speedy accountability but that would not cure the disease. It would be like aspirin that could provide temporary relief but never cures the cause of the headache. As long as the government head remains endowed with unbridled powers, derived from the law, custom or rules of business, the misuse of office would continue unabated notwithstanding the threat of accountability.

Instead of wasting time and energy on undoing the past wrongs, which is hardly possible, Gen Musharraf should concenrate on eliminating those rules and factors that embolden heads of government in Pakistan to play havoc with the law and state institutions.

Try as he may, Gen Musharraf would not be able to recover a penny of the defaulted loans. He can confiscate the assets of the defaulters, put them in prisons, disqualify them from politics, but the state exchequer would not be enriched. The default has only occured on the loans advanced by the state-owned banks. It means that most of the defaulted loans were secured on the strength of political influence and not on the feasibility of the project. There are cases where loans have been advanced on non-existent projects. It also means that default would continue to recur as long as the banks remain under the administrative control of the government. The defaulters and the persons responsible for advancing loans to them should get the punishment they deserve, but it would not cure the disease unless the banks were reformed administratively.

Gen Musharraf may be thinking of various measures to deal with the epidemic of loan defaults. However, a few things can be done immediately. A law should be promulgated to unseat the loan defaulters from the assemblies. The loan defaulters should not only be disqualified from contesting elections and holding any public office, but theys hould also be evicted from politics.

Though and unpopular decisions would be required to put the economy back on the rails. Gen Musharraf would find that it is not easy to brush aside the IMF conditions for releasing badly needed funds. The hike in petrol prices appears inevitable and GST has to be imposed despite the traders' defiance. These two measures would not endear the new chief executive to the people who are already suffering an unbearable economic crunch.

The interntional community would closely watch the state of our relations with India. It expects, and we have promised, to revive the process of Lahore Declaration. The dialogue could not be delayed for long. Indian Prime Minister Atal Behari Vajpayee has offered to talk with whichever government is in power in Pakistan. Gen Musharraf should accept the invitation and try to keep the dialogue process going.

The circumstances and stupidities of the politicians have burdened Gen Musharraf with great responsibilities. All power now flows from him. He should use this power only for the good of the country. He should focus ahead and avoid the pitfall of looking backwards which would only blur his vision and prevent him from the real task of nation building. His government should respect the human rights and carefully avoid any step towards abridging press freedom.

The politicians who have no representation in parliament and who have a scant chance of winning elections would like Gen Musharraf to prolong his stay. He should not be taken in by their plaudits. Their aim is to get their dirty work done by the army. They merely want to settle old scores with their political opponents.

I shall end this article by quoting a pearl of wisdom from Abaji. With tears in his eyes, Mian Muhammad Sharif told his visitors that his sons were suffering because they had defied him. He said that he had always advised them to avoid confrontation with the army. But Prevez Rashid (member of the suspended Senate and chairman PTV) was always pushing them against the army.

---

* Courtesy : *The Pakistan Times (Pakistan)*

28

New Admn Must Respect Public Trust

* *Nisar Ahmad*

Chief Executive General Musharraf Pervaiz's procrastination to promise a likely timeframe for holding elections seems sagacious on two accounts. First, this position of the CE is endorsed by majority of Pakistanis with high hopes for accountability of the previous rulers for corruption and mismanagement. And second, as one of his pronounced objectives, the course of the ongoing inter-provincial revulsion caused by the policies of the previous dull-witted and greedy politicians has to be reversed. It is of great significance that the subverted confidence for a working relationship between the four federating units be restored before we proceed to hold further elections. The process of Punjabisation of Pakistan instituted by the Nawaz government has to be cut out by the roots before the country can move on a normal track.

The composition of the new federal cabinet that has more representation of smaller provinces previously neglected by the ousted government authenticates that the chief executive is motivated to put the governmental business in order. To reverse the earlier government's unilateral acts that inflamed antagonism among the rest of the provinces against Punjab, the pronouncement not to construct the Kalabagh Dam without consensus is one more big step towards normalising and reinforcing the relationship between all federating units. These and other similar steps will add to the credibility of the new government and help keep up the crucial public support to help carry out its commitment.

In this context Gen. Musharraf Prevaiz's pronounced intentions of shoring up the economy, purging corrupt political elements and civil/military bureaucrats and creating an atmosphere of trust and confidence before committing himself to hold elections has, we think, substance of objectivity. And majority of the nation is unanimously supportive of this stance evident in its rife expression of gratitude when the news of October 12 takeover by General Pervaiz Musharraf rumbled. People did anticipate a forceful accountability and relentless purge of politicians for restoration of stability in all aspect of our lives and they must not be let sown this time.

What is more, the current circumstances affirm to the tragic reality that we, as a nation, suffer from an incisive dearth in our political hierarchy of workable elements. We have to invent a new political system to create new class of leaders that could provide a mechanism to pull the country out from the swamp it has been pushed into by transgressors of our power structure. To avoid further reverses, the ground realities in the realm of politics must not be left the same before we proceed towards restoring normal parliamentary system. By transforming the current political structure before next elections will save us our limited resources, time and above all public faith in the electoral process itself will be re-established. Our political history makes evident the absurdity of our political order and the duplicity of our political leaders that has been on display right from the era of our independence till this day. Figuratively speaking, we in fact never had a chance to build faith in democracy or pick its genuine guardians, a condition mandated and perpetuated during and after the imposition of Ayub Khan's 1958 martial law.

Ayub Khan was known as an able administrator and a shrewd general, who seized on international opportunities arising from the rivalries of the Cold War and manipulated them to his advantage. He established strong military and economic relations with the US and entrusted himself with preserving these ties, as he claimed, in the great interest of the armed forces. Thus, well before imposing martial law, Ayub Khan as the commander in chief of the army, meddled in governmental affairs and exercised broad control over its decisions. The US threw full support behind Ayub Khan as Pakistan became a full partner in US's quest to circle then Soviet Union in order to contain the spread of communism.

Ayub was the first General that behaved detrimental to the armed force's reputation as repugnant towards democracy and power hungry. While promising a speedy return to constitutional government, Gen. Ayub targeted "antisocial" practices that he thought were rampant in Pakistan and explained that martial law was needed to eradicate black marketeering, bribery, smuggling and hoarding from the society. He promised to eliminate "inefficient and rascals" from politics and corrupt officials from civil services. That's how he began building foundation to fulfil his own political ambitions. His high profile 'meet-the-people' activity was unitiated to pave way for his future political objectives. So were the land reforms he introduced which instead of targeting landlords to break their hold on politics proved a mechanism to supplicate their support or dominate them politically. For the same reason he amended the prevalent press and publication ordinance to stifle and shut down newspapers that posed a threat to his plans. He resigned in disgrace.

A civilian government under the popularly elected leader ZA Bhutto was established in 1971. Markedly, he uplifted the dispirited public morale after the 1971 debacle and strengthened ties with the oil-rich Arab countries that made possible mass labour emigration which brought back the much-needed foreign exchange. Bhutto however failed to break the power of the notorious 21 families that had emerged as dominant political and economic oligarchy during Ayub Khan's time. His socialism stunt did nothing for reforming the country politically or economically but surely helped him monopolise the decision-making power that in the end, except for a few closed friends, left him forsaken by everyone. Many believe that it was Bhutto's inflexibility on participating in dialogue to frame the new constitution that prolonged Yahya Khan's martial law, thus causing events which eventually led the country to disintegration.

Bhutto surprised the opposition by announcing the holding of general elections in March 1977. The aim was to catch the opposition unprepared and take control of the National Assembly but the opposition refused to accept his party's overwhelming victory and subsequently the army took over in July of that year under the command of General Ziaul Haq, who later hanged Bhutto.

Zia validated the nation's apprehension about the dilemma of non-navigable civilian governments giving in to ceaseless army interventions—a phenomenon that could lead Pakistan towards the status of a failed nation. Zia became a pawn in US hands. He promised the nation with elections within 90 days but ended up ruling the country for eleven years till his death in August 1988 in a still mysterious air crash. He played many practical jokes on the nation that included Islamisation and setting up of Federal Shariat courts, reintroducing Ayub Khan's basic democracy system, controlled democracy, referendums and partyless elections.

But the nation denounced him as the one who interrupted democracy, turned Pakistan into a front-line state to fight a proxy war for the US against the USSR in Afghanistan, lied frequently and broke promises, fomented sectarian hatred, ruined vital institutions and introduced, though inadvertently, the culture of Kalashinkov and drugs.

Frankly, if civilian governments in Pakistan deplorably failed to in stitutionalise and advance democracy as the nation expected, the armed forces punished the country by robbing it off whatever little democracy it had achieved under these administrations.

Behind this tragic state of affairs has always been the complicity of those few families that caught hold in Ayub Khan's era and now have grown into over three hundreds. While the public without protection waited for miracle to occur, the control of their destiny remained hostage to these forces. As a result the efficacy of primary institutions such as legislative body of the federation, the judiciary, a more orderly executive branch and a competent independent media, by altering their substance and configurations, had been oppressed and shattered repeatedly.

General Musharraf faces a formidable task of rounding the bend and restoring some sort of public confidence in these institutions, which might be a time-consuming and vigorous exercise. To reconstruct order and normalcy at public level and faith in country's institutions would require steps of immense courage and tenacity on the part of Gen. Musharraf and his team to prevail as well as masses' ability to exercise patience and placidity as a gesture of full support. The nation must continue assisting the current administration in its resolve to put the country back on its course. The public has the legitimate claim to be vigilant as the generals before Musharraf have lied and deceived the nation but his initial actions prove that we can trust his words on face value. Any internal pressure to accelerate accountability in order to return to parliamentary process will forthwith undermine the government ardency and determination and may lead to prematurely relinquishing the process of accountability altogether. That will throw us back to square one just to pick up the task some other day in future.

In our passions for democracy we need not be inclined to let the exploitative forces that have scraped together and strengthened grind us unchecked. They have knocked over our future and might steal the future of our coming generation. The nation ought to stand up and demand justice and join the current administration to speed up concrete steps to secure a bright future for our children. The US Russia, China, Japan, the European Union and Commonwealth countries, all have, one after the other demanded respect for parliamentary system and return to civilian rule. These demands are put for absolutely without taking into account the disturbing nature of events that led to the present situation. The US and European nation's calls have however less to do with our future welfare and more with their own national interests in the region.

The 1973 Constitution provide for a framework for the ordinary function of all the institutions an workable governing mechanism. What we need is to create sovereign judiciary, not submission to the executive branch that protects rights the rights of all citizens and uphold the sanctity of the Constitution. We need to put together a system where the prime minister is compelled to visit, respond to charges and explain maters to the parliament about public and those private deals that save good or bad consequences on public life. The freedom of press is crucial. The merits and demerits of all government actions concerning the welfare of the country must be allowed for debates in country's print and electronic media.

Gen. Musharraf and his National Accountability Bureau (NAB) a critical and arduous assignment as stated, to revive the economy and promote provincial harmony to purge the national institutional politics. This project should go concurrently with creating an example of the present administration's own record of righteousness.

Implementing forcefully the nationwide monitoring system promised might ensure an healthy and ethical performance of Musharraf's administration may instantly stop the drainage over a 100 billion rupees, which allegedly being usurped by official corruption every year. His administration's dedication, discipline professionalism Work methods and management, and the cullectivity of his own administration be a prelude to the establishment of a healthy economic environment that can lead to the setting up of true form of democracy.

---

* Courtesy : *The Frontier Post (Pakistan),* October 11, 1999

29

A Bright Chance Provided to Democracy

** Muhammad Kaleem*

People from all walks of life heaved a sigh of relief, when on 12th of October the Nawaz government was booted out. Everyone was happy at the ouster of a man, and his cronies, who was bent on ruining not only the state institutions but also the very fabric of the state.

God knows what would have happened if the military had not moved in quickly. Thanks to General Musharraf and his comrades-in-uniform that saved the nation from an impending civil war. And think who would have been the loser if the scheme, the ousted premier, had gone the way, had planned. You and me-the people, nay the masses in the words of our leaders, who have given him a massive mandate to rule us.

No one, but Nawaz himself, the self-proclaimed democrat, is responsible and be charged for pushing the very people, who have given him this elevation, to uncertain waters. He was like Muhammad Tughlaq who ruled India in the 13th century. Like Tughlaq Nawaz was too ambitious and wanted to be a despot ala Tughlaq's style. Both are to be held responsible for their falls. They are one and the same, but in one aspect. Historians say that Tughlaq was born before his times. Nawaz on the other hand, as a student of history I predict with a firm belief, would be remembered as a man born after his times

It is no use to cry over what had happened to us. The time is short and precarious. The only option now is to act, and act not only wisely and swiftly but judiciously and carefully, too. Let the law takes its course. And we start our journey afresh with new zeal and vigour for a prosperous future. Future is ours but we have to sit our house in order and the priorities chalked out.

Accountability of each and every sacred cow be held. The process must be clean and above board. Every Pakistani is interested to see those taken to task, who have looted this country with both hands. But it should not be discriminatory. Those generals who have been responsible for depriving this country of many things too be made accountable ala Hazrat Umar (RA)'s treatment of the greatest general of Islam Khalid bin Waleed (RA).

But punishment alone won't work, a single penny due to extracted out of those who have defaulted on bank loans even at the cost of leaving them him and dry. This is the only solution of Pakistan's economic problem, and the treatment defaulters best deserve.

And for making accuntability, clean and honest people are to be assigned the job. They must be people with good track record, no leniency and favouritism, and above all independent of pressure and influence. It should be carried in a way that the process becomes permanent and automatic.

The money amassed by corrupt bureaucrats and politicians through whatever way too be taken back. The people who have built large palaces and estates through illegal gratifications and smuggling be also taken to the task. And those who have made to power corridors through back doors be shown the door and properties confiscated.

This done, and the money thus collected be given to the debtors and the remaining amount allocated to the development of a agriculture and sick industrial units. We have rich and fertile lands that can grow three crops a year. The need is only to give proper guidance and the necessary tools, and a little hard work. And the revival of sick industrial units would then simply put us on the real road to progress.

Every one in Pakistan is aware that most of our problems are caused by low literacy rate. It needs to be enhanced on war footing. With wordly education religion too be taught and its spirit inculcated and enforced. Our miseries are mainly due to non-awareness from our religion. The education should not be only job-oriented, it should be character-based. Only good and sound education - having a solid religious background enables a people to distinguish between right and wrong. This trait of distinguishing between the right and wrong candidate we vote for is essential for democracy and a prosperous nation. And this comes through education.

The culture of taxation needs to be inculcated in this land of tax-evaders. Everyone has looted this country for long. Now is the time to return. Government for ever can not be run through borrowed money, we have to contribute to the national exchequer for the development badly needed by us all.

We have to shun telling lies and start speaking the truth. The time of day dreaming is over and we must, as in the words of Constantine Francois Volney : "Let us all seek truth as if none of us had possession of it". For a prosperous Pakistan with a flourishing democracy we have to be true to ourselves, to the nation we make and to the land we inhabit.

We have to go away with the laziness and lethargy that has sit upon us as a whole. The time for parties and functions be spared for sometimes else. Only hard work can make for the loss we have inflicted upon ourselves. Many things can be counted here, but for the sake of brevity and the short time at our disposal we can say that democracy has a bright future in a prosperous Pakistan provided; Across-the-board accountability is held in a transparent manner, and the looted money taken back and guilty taken to the task.

Literacy rate be made high through crash programs so that the voters know well that who they are electing to rule on their behalf.

Only people with clean track record, good education and character, and have good vision and vigour are chosen for the job. And above all those elected must have the leadership qualities and accessible to each and every one.

---

* Courtesy : *The Frontier Post (Pakistan)*, November 7, 1999

30

Political Agenda For The Nation

** Mian Ikhlaq-ur-Rehman*

When the whole world is preparing to enter the third millennium with their hopes solely resting on their progress, emancipation and prosperity, the unfortunate Pakistani Nation will have nothing but to shed tears over its tragic destiny and to shy away and slid silently out of the community of progressive nations who are marching over to the next era of prosperity, participation and freedom. All forms of unrepresentative government, monarchies, military dictatorships, feudalistic and aristocratic oligarchies or theocracies, do not go with the liberated human psyche of the present era and it is not an honourable asset for the dignity of the human beings to be ruled by a whip; only the governed have the right to govern themselves.

Though unwelcome, the military rule in Pakistan is not because of any ambition on the part of the army itself, but it is the folly of the civil institutions which have thrust it down our throats. For the last many years anarchy had been spreading in the civil institutions, lately reaching an acuteness which started gnawing the inner cordon of the Armed Forces, the only institution which had yet escaped its rampage. The stampede speed of the rushing anarchy demanded that of all the national agendas the agenda to save this vital institution should take priority. If the army had not moved in to save itself and the country in turn, the spreading anarchy which held the reins of all the civil institutions would have ripped it apart, with the commanders of our forces, the national ideals and role models, pulling at the cuffs and lapels of each other, rendering this institution crippled for ever as planned out by the external forces completing the hegemonial sway of the non-Muslim world over the globe, on the eve of farewell to the second millennium. Thus the non-Muslim world wanted to buy a safe passage for itself through the third millennium. The ousted political regime of the country, wittingly or unwittingly, became a tool in the process and the external forces tenaciously and strongly saddled on it steered it along pulling the reins so hard that its mouth bled.

Situational demand outlived the patience of the armed forces and they had to move in with a heavy heart, knowing it very well that the act did not fit in, anyway, with the modern concept of a progressive nation and would be considered by all as a regressive step. But here not only the destruction of the vital institutions of the country was on the anvil, the monopolistic managed democracy and patrimonial polity being practised in Pakistan, as I pointed in my article Liberal Democracy (The Pakistan Times 13-10-99) was in its bid to subjugate all the national organs annihilating the national character, which is a composite of all the national institution co-habiting in the national psyche and not a monotone and monochrome entity.

The time for a decision is there, the country cannot be left for long in an undecided situation, but at the same time no hasty decision can be taken on outside pressure. Formulae may be universal, but their application is specific to the area of application. We will have to give in time what is due to a proper decision. Any fault this time will leaves no room for any correction for ever in the future. The world pressure is mounting every moment for reversion to the old pattern. Pecunniary punishments are being proposed, pronounced, waved at and warned by the parent of the democratic system of governance. The government should not be distracted by any foreign pressure or by the volley of the foreign media. It should without alienating itself from the global brotherhood relatively concentrate more on bringing order on the home ground for it is after all where it has to launch the march of the nation. United States of America, European Union, Commonwealth and others speaking out their concern over the recent change in Pakistan should know this that we cannot play a viable and fruitful role in the world community if we have chaos amongst our social and institutional ranks. We have to bring order, so that the country can move on with all its sectors and institutions in unison. There are a number of ways for the participation of the people in the national affairs, but a desirable way has to be chosen keeping in mind the democratic, political and social environment of the country.

But, if the Patrimonial Polity is to continue then the whole exercise started by the Army will become totally futile, irrelevant, fruitless and a purposeless waste of the national sources in time and material. No doubt the Army which had moved in against a provocation and without any prior agenda is suddenly face to face with the formidable task of running the affairs of the State, still it is welcome respite if it provides time enough to the saner elements of the society to think out a viable political system for the country. The past of the country has been the field in which almost every representative system was tried, but the failures and the military takeovers brought out the faults and weaknesses of these democratic experiments. We should start with clearly defining the role of the institutions. The national and the provincial assemblies are legislative institutions, their purpose is legislation and not administration. Administration should be left out for the administrative head of the country i.e. the President, elected by the direct vote of the people to bring in his person the spirit of the people, and in his action the desire of the people. The President should appoint a non-parliamentarian as the Prime Minister, who in turn after approval of his appointment by the National Assembly, should take from the general public citizens to assist him as cabinet ministers in running the affairs of the country. The President elected by the direct vote of the people will be the will of the people, and the Assemblies will be the voice of the people on public and national issues. The resolutions of the assemblies shall be implemented by the President through the Administrative office of the Prime Minister. In matters of legislation the Assemblies shall have the absolute right. The Prime Minister and his cabinet, free of any electorate pressure, will smoothly carry out the national agenda laid down by the Parliament. The parliamentarians devoid of administrative powers, provided by law traditional or convention will not be able to exploit their position thus freeing the people of the schakles of patrimonial polity and Monopolistic Managed Democracy. Once the Prime Minister is appointed by the President and his appointed by the President and his appointment approved by the Parliament, then his removal would require an impeachment by both the legislative houses and its approval by the president. In case of any stalemete the Assemblies shall have the final say with a resolution backed by absolute majority vote.

With the present rift between the Political Head of the country and the Armed forces the idea of a National Security Council has come out loud and large. This council as an advisory body to the President, will watch and safeguard the vital interests of the country by not allowing any head of any institution to take any arbitrary decision detrimental to the overall purpose of the nation, and will bring in the force of unanimity of the country's vital institutions in every decision of the government, once and for all it will end the anarchy of the institutions present in the country. The National Security Council should have the following members:

1. President of Pakistan.
2. Prime Minister.
3. Chiefs of Three Forces.
4. Chairman of Joint Chiefs of Staff Committee.
5. Auditor General of Pakistan.
6. Heads of the Senate and the Assemblies.
7. Leader of Opposition in the Assemblies.

8. Defence Secretary.
9. Secretary Finance.
10. Chairman Planning Commission.
11. Chief Justice of Pakistan.

The political agenda requires some time for implementation. To begin elections should be held for the office of the President of Pakistan, who should appoint the Prime Minister after assuming the office of the President. Next the National Security Council should be established. The President, the appointed Prime Minister with his cabinet members and the National Security Council as an advisory body should run the affairs for at least two years, during which the process of accountability should be completed and then the elections to the National and the provincial assemblies held, finally establishing the new representative political system in the country, with the revival of the local government institutions.

---

* Courtesy : *The Pakistan Times,* October 26, 1999.

31

The Future Political Scenario

* *M.S. Qazi*

General Musharraf in a press conference on November 1 unfolded a plan to gain legitimacy for military take-over, military rule which he intends extending in a timeless frame and possibly for any array of measures which might change the form of government through a nation-wide referendum whose contours are yet to be defined and made clear. The proposed referendum is to be deliberated by the NSC before it gets a concrete shape of public vote.

Slow-paced development since the army, have cleared the haze over political spectrum of the country marginally to predict futuristic scheme of things to come which the chief executive would be obliged to unfold and execute to give concrete shape to his seven-point agenda he announced on October 17.

Taking over power by the army was sudden and abrupt. It was not a premeditated coup whose leader should have taken no time to unfold his plans in quick succession. Hence understandable delay. People of Pakistan accepted the change on October 12 in good faith as they did in 1958 and 1977. The US, the EU and the Commonwealth unlike in the past had initially some reservations. Their reservations have hardly been mitigated. Nevertheless they are willing to accommodate the coup and military rule for some time. Their reservations will continue to persist till Pakistan reverts to democratic dispensation and the army goes back to barracks.

Within the country, political parties, including Nawaz Sharif's PML, are waiting in the wings to clearly chalk out their future programme, even though some of them have conditionally supported the coup and others demanding restoration of democracy and strict ehtesab (accountability). The PPP has opted for the latter. The PML might move the Supreme Court against the military coup.

The PML has rejected the proposed referendum and constitutional amendments likely to be put forth by the CE. GDA's Nawabzada Nasrullah has opined that there was no need for referendum. He was seeking back-door entry to power when he said that politicians with good character be inducted in the government.

The National Security Council—a brainchild of the military—has been formed with four newly inducted civilian members. Their professional acumen and longstanding invaluable experience notwithstanding, they do not inspire public confidence for two reasons. First, they are unlikely to provide any dynamism and initiative at their own to the NSC; it would rest with the CE. Second, Dr. Yaqub and Pirzada are specialists in their own fields but the expertise of other two members—Dr. Atiya and Imtiaz—do not fit in the portfolios of foreign and national affairs which they occupy respectively. Hence the question, why are they there? Only to be counted or for something more subtle and specific than this?

The general consensus about the NSC members is that they are status-quo-oriented. Such an impression is certainly based on the contribution which they have hitherto made in national affairs, particularly to promote democratic institutions, rule of law and to put the economy on the right track. But, it would no take much time to put such a view-point to test. Their initiative, dynamism and contribution at this crucial national juncture should speak louder than their past.

The appointment of finance minister, Shaukat Aziz is being watched with mixed feelings keeping in view previous appointments of Moeen Qureshi and Shahid Burki who were 'imported' to straighten Pakistan's economic problems during caretaker governments. It is, however, to be appreciated that they had short duration of 90 days each to put the economic disorder in order. Keeping in view the gigantic task which they had to tackle, it could be observed that at least the first incumbent did succeed to implement somewhat sound changes in the economy which if pursued by the PPP government subsequently would have helped to revive the economy.

The finance minister faces a daunting challenge. He will have to work and produce result in a short time of 2-3 years to revive the economy on sound footing in an environment which will not be smooth in which he is accustomed to work. That is where real challenge to his acumen rests. He met IMF officials on October 30 to build bridges with them and his priorities are reported to be resolving IPPs issue, deregulating POL prices in accordance with international market trends and reforming tax administration. All these are included in IMF conditionalities.

The newly established Accountability Cell (AC) has replaced the Ehtesab Bureau. Press reports indicate that financial matters of sitting members of suspended National Assembly. Senate and other stalwarts of the deposed government are being investigated to determine irregularities committed by them. One only hopes that the cell makes investigations and the administrative and legal actions that would follow, transparent and across the board. Nevertheless, the new setup should pursue accountability process to its logical conclusion to prune corrupt political and bureaucratic heavyweights.

This is one specific area in which the government could show tangible results to the public and may win their support for extended stay in power in a timeframe which the CE is not ready to commit. Even EU Commission admitted her failure to elicit any time-frame from the CE.

The deposed prime minister is a 'natural' choice who will have to undergo stringent accountability to be initiated by the new administration. He is already under investigation. The CE in an interview with Abu Dhabi television is reported to have said that there are legal and financial matters and issues of corruption and then there are pressing demands from the Pakistani people regarding holding Nawaz Sharif accountable. "Let's allow justice to take its course... the investigation is undergoing to determine the issues that he was involved in and the extent of that involvement." The statement by the CE clearly indicated what lies ahead for Nawaz Sharif. But, it is equally important that not only he but Benazir Bhutto and others should also be held accountable in absolutely transparent accountability process.

The most sensitive question is about the timeframe to return to democracy. Also, associated with this are a number of other important questions such as fate of NA, Senate, scope of allowing the PML to elect new parliamentary leader, checks and balances of which the Constitution has been deprived and so on. Perhaps some of these issues will be addressed only after the envisaged referendum.

Gen Musharraf while answering the question regarding return to democracy said, "we certainly are not talking about months. But I do not want to comment on years". He further said that he was under 'no obligation' to give the world a definite date for his return to barracks. The general knows that he cannot play' no obligation' card repeatedly and for too long. That is why he is talking of referendum and after it, in all probability, it will be a matter of 'years'.

The Commonwealth and EU teams did not succeed to extract any timeframe from the CE to return to democracy. The former had offered two years to restore democracy. They also offered to extend co-operation in drafting a new constitution. Nevertheless such overtures had little bearing on the special circumstances in which the army was forced to take over and is to operate to restore normalcy and create environment in which democratic institutions could function effectively.

The emerging scenario clearly indicates that getting some sort of legitimacy for the military takeover, accountability and revival of economy are getting top priority. It will not be possible to achieve tangible results in last two fields in a timeframe of less than 2-3 years. The new setup whose contours have started unfolding, could have public acceptance. Will it succeed to correct multiple faultlines running into country's body politic which were partly created by the previous military rulers? Or, will more faultlines will be created by the new rulers in their bid to correct the old ones? Whatever the guess, the fear of long-drawn battle of wits between those who are in power and those who have been thrown out of power cannot be ruled out. It might not augur well for the country.

---

*Courtesy : *The Frontier Post (Pakistan)* November 8, 1999.

32

The Referendum Proposal

* *Mir Jamilur Rahman*

The idea to hold a referendum has not found favour with the major political parties. Chief Executive General Pervaiz Musharraf had proposed the referendum to acquire constitutional legitimacy for the army's rule and to seek public approval for the constitutional reforms, which he intends to introduce.

The political parties foresee dangerous complications in amending the constitution through a referendum. The PPP apprehends that this method of constitution-making would harm the federal structure. The PPP has demanded immediate restoration of the constitution, democracy, and representative rule. It favours the process of accountability but feels concerned at linking it with the restoration of democracy.

Raja Zafarul Haq, a senior PML leader, has termed the present military rule as the fourth martial law of the country. He is of the opinion that martial law does not solve problems. Instead, it complicates them and adds a few more. He said that no individual should attempt to tinker with the constitution because that would create more problems.

The Balochistan National Party (BNP) said that the October 12 action has dishonoured Pakistan. The country is now isolated and without a constitution. It sees the accountability as a means to denigrate the politicians. It has proposed a committee of pious judges to carry out accountability of the generals, politicians, bureaucrats, and traders from 1947. It has appealed to the political parties, especially the PPP, PML and ANP, to end their differences and unite for the restoration of the constitution and democracy.

The ANP has opposed holding referendum recalling the bitter experience of General Zia's referendum. The ANP said that it was unjustified to blame only the politicians for corruption and has demanded transparent and ruthless accountability of the armed forces, judiciary, bureaucracy, and the press.

Some PML leaders have suggested that the right forum for legitimising the actions of Gen. Musharraf would be the parliament. They have obliquely hinted that they have the numerical strength in the National Assembly to win legitimacy for the army's rule and if need be provide support for the constitutional amendments. The PML seems ready to work out this proposition without Nawaz Sharif. Obviously, the rest of the parties are deadly opposed to the revival because that would mean the reinstallation of the PML government though under a new prime minister. Gen. Musharraf is also not keen for the revival and has indicated that the National Assembly would die its own death with the end of its term in two years's time.

The referendum would be a double-edged sword. First, its legal and constitutional status would be challenged in the Supreme Court. Second, the political parties would demand public debate, some to canvass and others to oppose, the issue for which the referendum was being held. It would lead to public meetings, agitation, and street demonstrations for or against the issue. A military government cannot sustain political opposition and would therefore prefer a referendum without allowing a political debate. In that case, a favourable referendum result would prove worthless politically.

If the political debate were allowed, then who would speak for the military government? Granted that some political leaders have supported the idea of a referendum, but they would expect quid proquo to run a campaign for it on behalf of the military government. It would mean associating politicians in the military government, which is the last thing Gen. Musharraf would like to do. But he would soon discover that there is no escape from the politicians because his civilian cabinet, mostly composed of specialists and technocrats holding Ph.D. and MA degrees, has neither the inclination nor the experience of communicating with the people on the political level.

It has been stressed that the cabinet ministers inducted recently are highly educated and specialists in their fields implying that they would prove better in governance than the ill-educated politicians would. This premise is highly debatable. The government is not a university. The needs of the university are limited to qualified teachers and specialists who would prepare the youth for greater responsibilities. However, to run a government men of vision, statesmanship and political insight are required. The technocrats and specialists could perform well at the secondary government levels or in the thinktanks, but to expect them to create policies and then sell them to the people is asking for too much. They would not know how to talk to the people.

The traders have rejected the imposition of the GST threatening to go on strike if the decision was not withdrawn. The traders had forced the last government to withdraw the similar decision by observing a complete strike. Qazi Hussain Ahmed has termed the decision unpopular, cautioning that it would cost the military government people's support. He warned that traders might go on strike again, which could not be stopped by the use of force.

The chief executive has to take a few unpopular, but correct, decisions to revive the economy. However, such decisions, which include the price hike in atta and the expected rise in petrol prices, have to be put in the right perspective and explained to the people who ultimately would be the main sufferers. Similarly, the people have to be educated that the recovery of defaulted loans and government dues, which may run into billions, would not end their economic travails. Petrol prices would not come down, the electricity cost would keep on rising, and the prices of food and other items of daily use would not get stable in the foreseeable future.

The modern government is the product of politics. People may dislike the politicians, but they cannot do without them. The present policy of the government has created the impression as if it is a fight between the politicians and the rest. That is not so and should not be so. Gen. Musharraf should try to obliterate the impression that his government is in confrontation with the politicians as a class. Otherwise, it is probable that parties that are antagonists to each other, like the Muslim League, PPP, and the Jamaat-e-Islami, may join hands against him for the restoration of representative government.

---

* Courtesy : *The Pakistan Times,* November, 8,1999

33

Need For HR-Based Constitution

* *I. Kamal*

"They plot and plan, and God, too plans; but the best of Planners is God" - The Holy Quran, Sura Al Anfal, 8:30.

Praise be to God Almighty for delivering Pakistan from a ruthless dictator in the guise of a democratically elected leader, whose henchmen where about to send two hundred innocent men, women and children to a fiery death in order to get rid of a general he did not like. In the past, the Most Merciful has given repeated chances to various leaders of Pakistan to put the country back on the track, but the leaders have frittered away the chances through self-interest and abuse of power given in trust. That chance has just been given to General Pervaiz Musharraf, a sincere and honest professional on whom the country is now pinning its hopes. Once the corrupt and incompetent have been brought to task through ruthless accountability, a future set-up would have to be devised so that there can be no return to the plunder and loot which has beleadguered Pakistan for the last forty eight years.

The future setup must address the root cause of past instability which in this writer's opinion, are the following: although there were demonstrations of unity for brief periods just after its creation and during the 1965 war with India, the country has not been able to forge a national identity, and neither the parliamentary system of government nor the military dictatorships under which the country had been governed were able to deliver the goods.

A National Identity

"Woe unto the nation that is split into numerous fragments/ Each fragment considering itself to be a nation!" - Khalil Gibran.

One of the biggest impediments to progress and development in Pakistan has been its conversion into a multi-national state, with its major components at loggerheads. The concept of multiple nationalities is a negation of the Two-Nation Theory on the basis of which Pakistan was founded. Its logical conclusion is civil war or disintegration, as we have seen in the Balkans and the former Soviet Union, and as we learnt to our own sorrow in the case of Bangladesh.

The best way to get rid of the evil of multiple nationalities in Pakistan is to remove the ethnic connotation from the administrative divisions of the country. The Quaid-e-Azam had described the existing demarcation and the consequent provincialism as "a relic of the old administration". He had said, "We are now all Pakistanis—not Baluchis, Pathans, Sindhis, Bengalis, Punjabis and so on... and we should be proud to be know as Pakistanis and nothing else." (June 15, 1948).

The re-demarcation of provincial boundaries (which has been proposed by sincere and honest patriots like Air Marshall Asghar Khan), should be based not on ethnic lines but on administrative divisions small enough so that democracy can be felt at the grass roots. Such a delineation already exists in the form of the twelve former divisions of West Pakistan under One Unit. One Unit failed because of the true or imagined fear of domination by the Punjab. A 'setup where sixty percent of the population lives in one province is unwieldy, and is bound to raise feelings of insecurity in the smaller provinces (in contrast, the population of California, the largest state of the USA, is only fifteen percent of the country's population).

Many of the political squabbles in recent years emerged because of meddling by the federal government to enforce and strengthen its party's rule in Punjab, the most populous state. Restoring the former divisions of West Pakistan as provinces or states would avoid controversy and hassle, and provide all the benefits of One Unit without the disadvantage of the fear of domination by the Punjab.

Each of the twelve divisions have enough resources to develop and prosper. For example, the two divisions of Baluchistan, considered to be the most disadvantaged, have Sui gas, over which they should be given full control, and a long coastline, which can be developed with port cities and tourist resorts. The new demarcation would not detract from the heritage of any ethno-linguistic group, which did not suffer any cultural shock when the Hindu component was withdrawn in 1947, nor when the groups lived under One Unit for fifteen years.

The present provincial setup legitimises ethnic divisions, and results in problems of national significance such as the Kalabagh Dam issue to be viewed from the parochial point of view.

The new provinces should have the right to impose and collect their own taxes and spend the revenues within their own boundaries. The federal government should restrict itself to defense, foreign affairs, inter-provincial affairs, currency and a few other necessary portfolios. As in the USA, government and taxation should be, at three levels: municipal or district, state and federal. This will avoid squabbles which invariably occur over the allocation and release of funds by the federal government under the NFC awards.

No democracy is a true democracy unless it is felt at the grass roots, and it can only be felt at the grassroots by the devolution of power down to the district and municipal levels. With the twelve provinces, no leader would have grounds to exploit sections of the population on ethnic or parochial grounds, and the people would unite to fight the common enemy of injustice, corruption and the absence of meritocracy. Once the citizens of Pakistan cease to identify themselves on the basis of their ethnic origin, a sense of national identity as Pakistanis will emege.

A Tripartite System of Government

As Imran Khan had pointed out some time back, politics in Pakistan had become a business of istaking and making money. The only way in which this stigma can be removed is by removing the ilucrativeness from political office through a separation of the executive branch of government from the legislature. The parliamentary system of government is one of the worst legacies of British rule in the sub-continent. In the villages it has served only to legitimise feudalism. In his address to the joint session of parliament on December 2, 1989, ex-president Ghulam Ishaq Khan had accused the legislators of doing "everything but legislate". Obviously, they have not time to legislate when there is more attraction in becoming ministers and advisors, and being pampered by the leader of the house in order to retain their loyalty.

In an interview given a few years back, Sardar Ataullah Mengal had described the state of affairs in the following words : "The former Chief Minister of Baluchistan Zulfiqar Ali Magsi had only one seat for his own party, but he remained chief ministers for three years by giving ministries to all his coalition partners. People have been spoilt. In the current assembly, every MPA says that the awaam have given me a mandate to be a minister. In the previous government all members of the coalition were ministers. What's the problem with you? Why do you say that everyone will not be made a minister? They want to be ministers not to serve the people but to eat, drink and be merry".

It is sad and ironical that a few months after this interview Sardar Mengal's party had to succumb to the same process of political bribery in order to retain its hold on the government. India and Bangladesh, two other countries which have parliamentary democracies on the British pattern, do not lag far behind Pakistan in corruption. India's relative success is due to honest and sincere leadership during its formative years and the abolition of the feudal system. Whatever progress it has made has been achieved in spite of, and not because of, the parliamentary system of government. However, all is not well. The country has had five coalition governments since April 1996, and politicians are now struggling to put together a sixth one. Some prominent politicians such as Digvijay Singh (ex-governor of Madhya Pradesh) and Abdur Rahman Antulay (member of parliament) have called for a change in the system.

It is true that no system of government can be successful unless there is a desire to fulfil the spirit as well as the letter of the Constitution. However, the Constitution should provide safeguards such that the spirit of democracy cannot be broken, and power cannot be abused. In Pakistan, a constitution similar to the U.S. constitution is required with a system of checks and counter-checks provided by separate and autonomous legislative, judicial and executive arms of the government and a working president elected with the whole country as his or her constituency.

A country with limited resources cannot afford the luxury of figure-head presidents and figurehead governors. With the current setup in Pakistan, ministries are given out as bounties and the price for loyalty rather than as a administrative necessities. Under a tripartite system of government, the country's president and the elected governors of the provinces will be able to choose their cabinets from technocrats, social workers and people of learning who have no time for politicking.

The country can hardly expect to succeed unless it puts it first eleven to bat, chosen not on the basis of kinship or affiliation but on sheer merit. With ministers chosen from competent experts in the related fields and not from the legislators, there will be no incentive for the party in power to increase the ministers and advisers to ridiculously high numbers which adds to the burden on the country's economy. The role of the legislators is to serve as a permanent accountability commission and as watchdogs over the executive branch.

The achievement of these ends, which will make the task of governance easier for whichever party is elected to power, would require a new constitution. The old constitution had been mutilated to bits anyway by Zulfikar Ali Bhutto and the unworthies who succeeded him. The military leaders of Pakistan have the opportunity to give the country a new constitution based on fundamental human rights and the foundations necessary for good governance.

---

* Courtesy : *The Frontier Post (Pakistan),* November 13, 1999.

34

Governance in a Political Vacuum

* *M.S. Qazi*

The quasi-military coup on October 12, like other military coups in Pakistan in the past or elsewhere in the world created political vacuum in the country. This time instead of imposing martial law to fill in the political vacuum, the vacuum has been filled in through a loose civil-military setup which of course is no replacement for a political order. The new civil-military setup has the backing of military. The civilians in the new setup do not have an entity of their own. Providing good governance for keeping the legitimacy and credibility of the coup through unspecified timeframe in a political vacuum, is the biggest challenge which the CE faces.

The coup-makers rationalise their take-over and staying in power on three accounts: the government of deposed prime minister was inefficient and did not deliver, Nawaz Sharif had tried to politicise the institution of army which was unacceptable to the army high command and lastly there was 'sham democracy' which needs to be replaced by 'genuine democracy'. The CE has laid down a lengthy and time-consuming seven-point agenda without committing himself to any timeframe. His evasive and reluctant attitude for not giving a timeframe to restore democracy is understandable keeping in view Gen Zia's promise of holding elections within 90 days which he did not fulfil and the multifaceted difficulties which the CE might be facing at present after assuming power.

The CE has raised an administrative edifice to give a direction to governance. The visible pillars of the new setup are NSC (National Security Council), NAB (National Accountability Bureau), NRB (National Reconstruction Bureau) the federal and provincial cabinets headed and manned by retired/serving generals and a few civilians. By now sufficient time has passed and as anti-Nawaz Sharif euphoria of non-performance which reached the highest crest on October 12 subsides, the performance of NSC, NAB, NRB and cabinets will come under public scrutiny. Unless the public scrutiny - a constant phenomenon - remains on a positive note, the legitimacy of October 12 quasi-military coup and efficacy of visible pillars of the new civil-military setup will be brought into question, at least on moral grounds if not on de jure and de facto grounds.

The NSC is the brainchild of the army high command which was publicly articulated by the former COAS, Jehangir Karamat about an year earlier. It was disfavoured by the deposed prime minister. The two did not see eye-to-eye on establishing it. Nawaz Sharif did not feel its necessity in the presence of DCC. In fact he did not revive the NSC, established during the interim government in 1997. The army wanted NSC to have its say at the policy and decision-making stage at the highest level. It was a sort of arrangement to share power between the civil and military establishment despised by the politicians. Now NSC is in place with all the power in the hands of the army.

To start with, the NSC is a non-starter on two accounts. First, the selection of members has been unconvincing. The members have a tilt towards the establishment and favour the status quo. One of them, Dr. Yaqub Khan was controversial for his role in taking the economy to the present state as governor SBP. He resigned in view of mounting criticism in the press and presumably because of the altercation between him and the finance minister on some of the decisions taken by the former as governor SBP.

Secondly, a member who sits in the NSC because of the 'liking' which is an essential requirement for objective decision making of the CE, could ill-afford to speak his/her mind independently as is obvious because of past eight weeks experience. Therefore, a hand-picked NSC hardly serves any national purpose. No one has heard, so far, of any contribution made by any of the NSC members. Surprisingly, no official reasosn was assigned to the resignation given by Dr. Yaqub Khan.

If the army high command had visualised an NSC with such role and composition of its members, it was not a enviable proposal. Presently, the chairman of NSC, the CE by virtue of being COAS is calling all the shots. Will the military let an elected PM call all the short as does the CE today, if NSC is established in a pure civilian setup with the political backing of the electorate? How would civil and military establishment share power? Where would the parliament stay? These are pertinent questions to be addresed.

NAB and NRB are in embryonic state. It might be a bit pre-mature to comment on their performance. But, a few pertinent points about them would not be irrelevant. NAB has an important task of nabbing those who have looted national wealth. Its job is tedious, laborious and time-consuming. Hopefully, it will be given the required leeway in discharging its responsibility but its performance will be judged on two accounts. First, its efforts are not directed against Nawaz Sharif and Benazir Bhutto alone. Second, after much hard work how much defaulted money it would recover and how many 'big fish' would be brought to book. Within next few weeks NAB would be either establishing or losing its credibility. It is already locking its horns with country's banking sector.

NRB is yet to let her presence felt to the nation. Her role would be advisory and working mostly academic. In a society and government irrespective of its being a political or military government, hinged on power structure with very little tradition and regard to academics, NRB has little role to play. Huge bureaucratic drag is enough to consume any of its recommendations, howsoever practical they might sound.

Governance is not administration alone. It requires a political medium to sustain itself and improve upon its quality subject to the condition of political system having institutional strength to keep check on those who are entrusted with power. The military coup has set up its symbols of administration - NSC, NAB, NRB, governors and cabinets - on top of the civilian administrative hierarchy with a view to monitoring and directing them but it is yet to motivate the civil administration to deliver effectively. Can governance at the turn of millennium sustain in political vacuum even for a short span of few years? The answer is negative.

Experience of three martial laws clearly indicates that martial law administration could not be sustained in political vacuum. Ayub Khan reverted to basic democracy and conventional Muslim League and so did Zia. General Musharraf cannot hold on in a political vacuum for too long. He has to revert to a political system, whether it would be 'sham democracy' or 'genuine democracy' that is besides the point. He has indicated that by the end of next year, local body elections would be held and there will be devolution of power. The basic question is: who would lead local leader? Will it be civil bureaucracy topped by military bureaucracy? If so, it would be an incoherent integration which would result in visible and invisible administrative friction.

Political forces in the country still exist. PPP and PML (N) are the major political forces. Their vote banks to a greater extent are intact notwithstanding their disillusionment with their leaders and governments. Other smaller political and regional forces are also staying intact. The poor governance of PPP and PML (N) government might have disenchanted the common man with the politicians and they might be looking forward that a political setup capable of providing good governance should be placed by the army at the helm of affairs. This is the role which they want the army to play in the shortest possible time and nothing beyond that. All political parties are unanimous in a political role of the army.

The present civil-military setup cannot work for too long in political vacuum. The military establishment must seriously work through a dialogue with the political forces to institutionalise a system of checks and balances to check bizarre love for power of the politicians and let the political forces and institutions function. There are a number of options which could help the government and political forces to steer the country out of the present crisis. The worst would be to rule the country in political vacuum for too long.

---

* Courtesy : *The Frontier Post, (Pakistan),* December 13, 1999.

35

The Nation Without Options: A Gender Perspective

* *Farzana Bari*

It is ironic that those who have always upheld the principle of social justice and democracy are in a state of paralyses and do not know how to react to the recent political development in the country. The duality of feeling has been pulling the selves apart. There is an inevitable sense of relief among genuine democrats on the overthrow of democratic dictatorship of Nawaz Sharif. Because during his rule, increasing poverty, high unemployment, hyperinflation, inaccessibility of basic goods and services, rampant corruption, plundering of national resources and increasing violence had made a life of an ordinary citizen a living hell. So much so that the Senate of the so-called democracy issued a licence to kill women in the name of honour on 2nd August 1999 when it prematurely killed a resolution in Samia Imran's case who was murdered by her family in the name of honour.

Nevertheless, in principle, all this does not justify an illegal and unconstitutional intervention of army in the politics of the country. Social scientists and political analyst can not turn a blind eye to the fact that the poor state of today's democracy in Pakistan is partly due to frequent interruption of democratic process in the country by the military dictatorships. The army has no constitutional right to interfere in political matters. However, the ground realities of the countries has coloured people's perception and obscured their reaction and response to the coup at this time.

The nature of politics, character of politicians and their track record in politics of the country has made democracy a dark tunnel for the nation. Politicians have betrayed people time and again. Consequently people lost hope and faith in politicians (not in political processes). Due to absence of any political option at the moment, this coup or counter coup did not meet any resistance from the civil society. However, this will be a mistake to assume that the civil society has given a mandate or a verdict in favour of military rule by being silent.

It is a national tragedy that presently; one can not propose or demand alternatives within democratic space. Demand for the restoration of elected assemblies will bring back plunderers and looters of national resources. Demand for holding fresh elections will pave way for corrupt politicians to the corridors of power. So what is left for civil society to demand within democratic space? The complexity of the political situation has been responsible for the lull in social reaction. However, civil society cannot afford this protracted silence. People must voice their concerns, protect and guard their rights and interests. Now, it is a challenge before civil society to shape its response without wasting any more time to the present political situation of the country.

While formulating position on military intervention in politics and its future relationship with present rulers, civil society should take into account women's point of view. It is important to understand that women, who subscribe to women's perspective(s), the issue of legitimacy of space is critical in order to participate in political processes. Although women's representation has been insignificant in the polity; however, they have been consistently trying to carve a space for themselves within mainstream formal politics. One of the strategies has been the demand for the reservation of seats in the political bodies at the national, provincial and local levels through affirmative action by the state. The emergency in the country has brought their struggle for enhanced political participation to an end. Women do not want to occupy any space within an arena that is inherently non-democratic and authoritarian. Under the circumstances, while women will be willing to engage themselves with military rulers to build up pressure on the government to deliver and ensure the restoration of fundamental democratic rights of people, they will not like to become a direct part of this set-up. Thus authoritarian rule by the army even if it is out of necessity pushes women out of political arena in totality.

Also, women are cognizant of the fact that non-democratic rulers who lack legitimacy always look for a unifying factor and use it politically for their own survival. In the past, military regimes have used religion for this purpose. Non-elected rulers always try to cater to popular ideologies that are very often patriarchal. Therefore, there is always a danger that in their zeal to become popular, they may tighten control over women's sexuality to appease the traditional element in society.

Keeping in view the above-mentioned points, the civil society has to suggest ways and guide the military rulers to take steps to democratize the processes they intend to undertake in order cleanse state structurer and rebuild a sound social and economic order during their temporary, short out of necessity stay in power. It is imperative for the credibility of the present rulers to be seen by the public as objective and genuinely committed to social justice. One of the major steps in this direction could be that the army should bring itself in the net of accountability. Kick back in the purchase of armaments by the army is part of common sense and people know that army is not above the board. It is important that military ruler should not be selective in their accountability drive and should have the courage and willingness to take it across the board.

Similarly, the nation has suffered due to wrong priorities by our national governments. Pakistan has been spending a meager percentage of its GNP on social sector. The major chunk of the budget is used for debt servicing and on defence. Without reducing defence budget and redirecting it towards social sector development, Pakistan does not stand a chance to emerge out of this social and economic disaster. It is also important that the role of army is redefined in the light of new realities of Pakistan as a nuclear power. If military rulers are serious to uplift the country then they must see and act beyond their own vested interest. They must ask and debate questions such as do Pakistan need to keep such a huge army that consumes a major share of its resources? Can Pakistan afford a standing army or the army should have more productive roles?

Military rulers need to work with a team of honest professionals, experts, and visionaries to chart out the plan for reconstruction of the country and give a time frame for the implementation and achievement of results. The selection of people in the Security Council has already disappointed those who were genuinely banking on army for their salvation. The basis for the selection of the members of Security Council should have been only their professionalism and excellence in their expertise. The top layered technocrats, bureaucrats, academics and professionals can not be trusted anymore, as they are too well known to the public for their political affiliations and compromises. The army should look for its team members from the second layer of professionals in different fields who have the reputation of honesty and excellence. These are the people who might be able to serve the nation.

It is critical that the civil society shapes its response and clearly defines what should be the role of the military and for how long they should stay in power and how they should make a shift towards restoration or real democracy in the country. The failure on the part of civil society to assert itself may darken the future of democracy in the country forever.

---

* Courtesy : *The Pakistan Times,* November, 10, 1999

36

Accountability of Nation

** M. Zahid Iqbal*

The process of accountability has once again caught the attention of the Pakistani people. The nation is eagerly awaiting the day when all loan defaulters and corrupt officials will be hunted down and the economy will be revived with the billions of rupees recovered from these people. Once again we have found a messiah who is magically going to deliver us from all the problems we face today as a nation.

However, as the initial euphoria over the overthrow of a corrupt government settles, Pakistani historians and journalists have already started pointing out the similarities between this exercise in accountability and those carried out by previous governments such as that of President Ayub Khan. It is being claimed that since nothing has changed so far, we are destined to revert to the inefficient and corrupt political system of government that General Pervaiz Musharraf replaced.

Pakistan's dilemma is that after having overthrown numerous successive corrupt governments, we still seem to have no shortage of corrupt and inefficient political leaders willing to replace the deposed rulers. However, having a very short attention span and a for giving disposition, the Pakistani nation is content with these temporary accountability campaigns. In fact, we are so forgiving that in the case of Benazir Bhutto and Nawaz Sharif, we have given them more than one chance to clean up their acts. Yet, we are once again seeing history being repeated as the threat of a death penalty haunts the newest victim of our accountability campaign. The man who overwhelmingly won the people's support only a few years ago now sits in a small, dark jail cell, while we criticise everything he did during his tenure as our leader.

In their enthusiasm to bring the political elite to justice, however, the new government and the general population have once again failed to mention a different kind of accountability that each and every citizen of Pakistan must face. It involves fulfilling the responsibilities that come with being a member of a free nation, and which every Pakistani must be held accountable for, regardless of their economic, political, or social status.

The inefficiency and corruptness of our political leaders seems to have had one obvious effect on the Pakistani nation. We Pakistanis, from our esteemed journalists to our simple citizens, have become masters of criticism. We criticise the fact that our politicians are corrupt, inefficient, and insensitive. We criticise them for failing to control violence. We accuse them of foolishly obtaining foreign loans and flagrantly squandering the nation's wealth. However, if we observe our own behaviour as common citizens of Pakistan, we will find the very same ailments inflicting us. The Pakistani nation loves to live beyond its means, even if that requires obtaining huge loans. An efficient and courteous public servant is an extinct species in our country. We lament the rise in violence and robberies committed by the younger generation, yet we place such huge financial burdens on our young adults to satisfy our archaic traditions that they are left with no choice but to transform into dacoits and robbers. Obviously, our political leaders hail from the same crowd. So why are we surprised when they spend the taxpayers' money and obtain foreign loans to live beyond their means? Why do we get upset when they hire and fire people at will? After all, our politicians are doing on a grander scale what we love to do each and every day in Pakistan.

Problems such as human rights violations, child labour, religious and ethnic intolerance inefficient and discourteous workers, corruption, and abuse of women and children have become ingrained in our society. It would be foolish to assume that by replacing a handful top politicians we can eradicate these social problems. More importantly, it would be unfair to our current and future political leaders for us to assume that they can get rid of all economic and social evils corrupting our society by simply amending our Constitution or changing our political system. Although our government does need to spend more on social programmes, it would be impossible to bring about the radical social and ethical changes that our society needs unless the Pakistani nation is willing to do its part.

One of the charges levied against Nawaz Sharif is that he had turned into a virtual dictator. However, no one is willing to accept responsibility for allowing Nawaz Sharif to turn into a dictator. In fact, it was the apathy of the Pakistani nation that allowed him to become a dictator. It would be naive to think that only a handful of Sharif's closest associates were responsible for the corruption and abuse of power rampant in his government. The fact is that thousands of Pakistani citizens contributed to Nawaz Sharif's success by remaining silent spectators to his abuses.

We as a nation have often decried the lack of basic human rights in Pakistan. However, we fail to understand that rights come with responsibilities. When members of a nation fail to fulfil their responsibilities, they forgo their rights. If the educated citizens of Pakistan do not fulfil their responsibility as voters then they have no right to criticise an inefficient government that comes to power by buying votes of the poor and uneducated. If we remain quiet when witnessing violence then we have no right to complain when we ourselves become targets of violence. It we abuse power and make life miserable for people belonging to a lower economic or social class, then we have no right to complain when someone more powerful than us tramples on our rights.

Obviously, in any nation, responsibilities are related to the status of each citizen within that country. An uneducated, poor farmer cannot be held accountable to the same standards as an educated bureaucrat. In developed nations, a major proportion of the population is comprised of the educated middle class, whose members hold significant influence over the government and help shape the destiny of the nation. In developing nations, however, the educated middle class is far outnumbered by the lower-income and uneducated class. Therefore, the responsibilities of the educated middle class increase significantly in developing nations like Pakistan. Unfortunately, the middle class of Pakistan has failed miserably in playing any role. The participation of the middle class in the electoral process has always been dismal, allowing the politicians to buy the votes of the poor and the uneducated. To make matters worse, the middle class has exploited the poor to imitate the extravagant lifestyles of our corrupt politicians.

If we are to emerge as a democratic and progressive society, we need to educate our citizens as to their rights and responsibilities. More importantly, we need to radically change the way we are raising our younger generation. Throughout their childhood and academic careers, young Pakistanis are taught never to question authority. In the name of respect, they learn never to question decisions made by their parents or teachers. How can we ever expect these Pakistanis to grow up and question their political leaders? Our society willingly encourages illiteracy among the poor so that we will always have cheap labor available. Today, millions of young children are being used as servants in our middle-class households, and are being denied an opportunity to educate or train themselves for a better future.

However, our shortsightedness has kept us from realising the ramifications of our actions. Pakistan's political leaders have often boasted of abundant humanpower available in Pakistan. However, in today's technological world an uneducated and unskilled worker is of no use. Similarly, Pakistan's abundant natural resources can be of no use if we do not have skilled labour and technology to utilise these resources. Although, the government is primarily responsible for providing educational facilities, given Pakistan's economic conditions, it should be the responsibility of every educated Pakistani to work towards eliminating illiteracy. Pakistan needs dedicated and honest citizens as much as it needs honest politicians.

Unlike a dictatorship, democracy cannot be imposed upon a nation. The level of democracy enjoyed by a country is a reflection of how enlightened and responsible that nation is. Unless the Pakistani nation is willing to cleanup its act, any person elected democratically to lead our nation will, willingly or unwillingly, eventually turn into a dictator. Maybe the time has come for us to hold the Pakistani nation partly accountable for Pakistan's misery.

---

* Courtesy : *The Frontier Post (Pakistan),* December 17, 1999

37

Look Out for the Traps

** Arshad Islam*

This is a wild country. The inclination to seek self-interest at the cost of all else has become an inherent psyche of the individual in particular, and the group in general. Unscrupulous political orators subjecting the gullible illiterates masses to visions of bright sunshine and plentiful have drained moral values. The common man has seen so much disillusionment in his lifetime that he has hardened himself to disregard the inner voice or moral behaviour. Given the opportunity today, the man in the street will resort to any illegality if it gratifies his needs or supports his survival.

He is now so demoralized after fifty years of relentless toiling and enduring the merciless evisceration of his rights, that he has no hope from the exploitive system and selfserving governments to promote his own and family life. It has driven him to exercise the animal instinct of self-preservation is respective of the right or wrong in the process.

Curb side policemen, the peon at the officers door, the lineman, the ticketing clerk, the meter reader, the bank teller, even the municipal janitor or sweeper will apply methods to extract the pound of flesh from his hapless quarry-the common man. Its man-eats man nearly. Each of these lowly servants of the public unashamedly mulct the citizen for whatever he can get in order to make his survival possible. The phenomena is all pervasive from top to bottom in the public and private sector.

With rising of the new sun in the garb of the Chief Executive, General Pervaiz Musharraf, there is going to be a deluge of íhonest, upright expertsî ready to render their ìextra-or-dinary high quality serviceî for the ìnationís goodî and to íenhanceî the chief executiveís national and international image. There will come to the court of Ra Pharisee dressed in resplendence to eruditely present their case for the ígood of the peopleî. Among them will be the snare of the political parties. People pleading in words of ìeternal wisdomî as independent thinkers, technocrats and talismen revolting against the treachery of the past government and proclaiming the merits of the present in order to get a foot in the door for their hidden patrons and mentors nationally and internationally. These are the traps. It has happened all the time with every new government. The traps are so complex nebulous, devious and ornate that very often they defeat investigation. The chief executive may have shown uncanny intelligence in recognizing the traps by his proclamation of a prayer the vision to see and perceive the truth from the false. Great prayer, great asset to get a handle on the traps.

In Pakistan we are beset with some of the most extra-ordinary and often intractable cause of failure. Distrust and despondency being in highlight. People have just lost faith in the leadership. They pursue a degenerated power of short-lived selfinterest simply because the failure of the systems put in place to serve them have in fact disillusioned them. We may have crossed the edge over the precipice already; yet hope must take precedence. Unless mistrust and despondency are replaced by hope and faith, the monumental efforts that the CE will put in are not likely to materialize. When people have hope in a better future, they repose trust and faith in the leadership. These qualities in turn create progress. Political orators have over the years vitiated the environment. Once that faith and trust are established, people will willingly contribute to the cause of the national development even if it means a great sacrifice.

Leadership is often drowned in the quagmire of inaction by the traps even before the initiation of concrete and bold steps for development are planned. How indeed does one establish an all-honest NSC, a ministerial panel below that and the operational bureaucracy subordinate to that and the monitoring set up further down and so on without having the monsters of the traps infiltrate at some tier to disrupt and put into disrepute the whole process of development. The Chief Executiveis first promise rebuild national confidence and morale is possibly the most urgent yet the most difficult of the promise. Structuring multi-tiered accountability and transparency is a gigantic task fraught with dangers of the traps. Ruthlessness is not synonymous with injustice. Transparency and speed in accountability can often detract from the quest for justice and without justice accountability has no meaning. Those to be entrusted with the task of accomplishing accountability and their layers of subordinates need to be clean themselves and must understand the concept behind the act. The outer fringes of the structure could unfairly apply the process to achieve their own personal ends, hidden vendetta, to cover their closeted shortcomings and their bitterness against individuals or institutions of the past. The ex-IG Sindh is a prime example of a structural element at a very high level going astray. This happens to be one aspect of the whole picture of reform envisioned by the CE. Every aspect—the economy, the administration, justice etc. are all-open to infiltration at some level by trappers. The stakes are so high for some of the major political parties that there is no chance of their desisting from implementing traps within the New Horizon plans of General Musharraf. As a thorough professional army man he must rely on the combined wisdom of the Army Command to identify and choose correct members of the many tiers in the process enabling them to design their subordinate platforms to match the rigorous specifications of the Chief Executiveís vision. I suppose it is possible for the multi-tier structure to be virus-free but I doubt it so I shall fall back on the Chief Executive enlightened prayer.

The traps are corrosive self-propelling, evasive and pervasive virus. They are short-fused to detonate progressive development in favour of their masters. The country does not matter to traps - the mission end does. Superior achievement of the present regime can only but further damage the image of past corrupt governments and political parties. They cannot risk such an eventuality, so they must relentlessly pursue the objective of disrupting the vision and future achievements of the present leadership. Beware of the traps. Those groups and individuals already toying with the notion of traps against the interest of the Nation are playing foul on the national scene so the whistle is blown.

---

* Courtesy : *The Pakistan Times,* October, 19, 1999

38

Accountability Juggernaut

* *Mir Jamilur Rahman*

The leader of the Pakistan People's Party, Benazir Bhutto, has described the National Accountability Bureau (NAB) Ordinance as 'draconian'. In this context she sees no difference in the policies of the present regime and those of Nawaz Sharif. Her contention is that the military's goodwill will evaporate if the people of Pakistan starts thinking that one dictator has replaced another dictator; that one vendetta has been replaced with another; and that the accountability bureau headed by a senator is now being headed by a general. In her opinion the 'blanket persecution' makes the accountability process controversial. "The people of Pakistan," she said, "want bread and butter, and not innocent blood."

Benazir Bhutto has expressed no confidence in the current accountability drive because NAB has declared her a proclaimed offender and fugitive from law. According to her the executive has no authority to take such an action because that authority rests with a court of law.

However, General Pervaiz Musharraf has no choice but to try a major surgery to cleanse the cancer of corruption that has been progressively eating into the vitals of the country. The all-pervasive corruption has produced bad governance, arbitrary rule, massive abuse of power, violation of human rights, and rampant lawlessness. The politicians and the bureaucrats considered it their right and privilege to live off the state to the extent of dooming the country's economic future.

NAB would serve a practical purpose. It is the only hope for the accountability of our politicians and bureaucracy who though blame each other for the bad governance but work in tandem to plunder the meagre resources of the country. The accountability process that was launched by the popularly elected leaders Benazir Bhutto and Nawaz Sharif was aimed at destroying the other politically. It was driven by their passion of revenge and political victimisation. While they hounded each other on charges of corruption, they remained oblivious to the sea of corruption that was engulfing them from all sides.

Gen. Musharraf's accountability process is of another kind. It has no likes or dislikes. It does not distinguish between an enemy and a friend. It is cruel because it encircles politicians, government servants, armed forces personnel, traders and industrialists. It is devoid of the faculties of sight, smell, and hearing. It has no respect for pedigree. This accountability process is akin to an operation theatre, painted white, laden with antiseptic smells, neutral in appearance and substance and the surgeon ready to try his skills to save the patient. If the surgeon did not try, the patient will die. If the surgeon tried and failed, the patient will die. Therefore, it is important that the surgeon must try.

The persons who have so far been charged or nabbed under the NAB ordinance represent the elite of Pakistan. There are two former prime ministers, three former chief ministers, one ex chief of the navy, one retired air-marshal, one retired major-general, one retired brigadier, several former federal and provincial ministers, and members of the suspended parliament and provincial assemblies.

Malik Asad Khan, the youngest son of the late Nawab Kalabagh, is in for loan default. Nawab Kalabagh was the governor of West Pakistan province, the present day Pakistan. He was an absolute ruler but did not allow his sons to come near the Governor's House as long as he lived there, which was pretty long. In contrast the family members of the deposed prime minister and the Punjab chief minister were free to exercise government authority on their own. A letter signed by Hamza Sharif has come to light. The letter typed on the chief minister's stationery tells a government functionary to carry out the order immediately. Mr. Hamza Sharif warned that he would not listen to any excuses pointing out that he was least interested to know whether his order was legal or illegal.

Mr. Jafar Leghari, first cousin of former president Farooq Leghari, has also been nabbed for loan default. Mr. Farooq Leghari, now chief of the Millat Party, has been vehemently advocating 'cruel accountability' least expecting that his kith and kin would also be subjected to 'cruelty'. NAB may also examine the helicopter case that was processed by a committee of the National Assembly. It was alleged that on the insistence of Mr. Leghari, then president of Pakistan, advance payment for the import of a helicopter was made to his brother-in-law, another son of Nawab Kalabagh. It may not be illegal to pay in advance except that the helicopter was never delivered.

Anwar Saifullah Khan of PML (J), a former minister who has served in the cabinets of both Nawaz Sharif and Benazir Bhutto, has been arrested on yet to be disclosed charges of corruption. He is son-in-law of the former president of Pakistan, Ghulam Ishaq Khan. He is related either by blood or marriage to some of the influential families of the NWFP including that of Field Marshal Ayub Khan, Aslam Khattak, and Lt. Gen. (R) Ali Quli Khan.

The arrests continue and may touch the figure of 50 very soon. It would be a formidable task to try this large number. The evidence has to be gathered and produced and proved in the court. The 30-day completion period of the case as provided in the NAB ordinance is an impractical proposition. The drafters of this stipulation know it. The law tells the court to finish the case in 30 days but is silent on what follows if for one reason or the other the deadline is not met. Will the case collapse and the judge punished for not meeting the deadline?

It would besmirch the credibility and legitimacy of the military rulers if they tried to rush the cases through courts like summary trials. The persons charged should be afforded full facilities to defend themselves. They should have free access to their lawyers and documents pertaining to their respective cases. And above all every conviction should go through the process of stiff judicial scrutiny.

It is a welcome statement that the government will sort out cases of wilful default and the default forced by circumstances beyond one's control. This differentiation is imperative otherwise the nascent corporate culture in Pakistan would collapse irredeemably. Moreover, the bankers who have advanced loans on considerations other than the sound feasibility of the project, or have advanced inflated loans not commensurate with the cost of the project, should be made co-accused in the default cases.

---

* Courtesy : *The Pakistan Times,* November 26,1999

39

The Screw Tightens

* *Mir Jamilur Rahman*

For the second time in the short history of Pakistan a former prime minister has been charged with crimes that carry the death penalty. The first, Zulfikar Ali Bhutto, met his fate at the gallows. The second, if the charges made against him are proved, may also end up there. Allah in His infinite wisdom acts in mysterious ways. The Sindhi prime minister was tried in Lahore and the Punjabi prime minister's trial is set for Karachi.

The first information report registered against Nawaz Sharif is quite comprehensive. The five complaints contained in the FIR emanate from one act: the denial of landing to the PIA flight in which Chief of Army Staff General Pervaiz Musharraf and 200 other passengers were travelling from Colombo to Karachi.

Besides Mr. Nawaz Sharif, his four aides have also been named in the FIR. They are: Syed Ghous Ali Shah, former adviser to the deposed prime minister on Sindh affairs; Rana Maqbool Ahmed, former inspector-general of Police, Sindh; Shahid Khaqan Abbasi, member of the suspended National Assembly and former chairman of PIA; and Aminullah Chaudhary, former director-general of the Civil Aviation Authority. Incidentally, the co-respondents in Bhutto's case were also four in number, all policemen. They were all sentenced to death and hanged.

The FIR cites the five accused for several crimes including attempted murder (maximum 10 years); hijacking (maximum death, forfeiture of property and fine); kidnapping or abduction (maximum 7 years and fine); and criminal conspiracy (maximum death). Most probably, the accused would be tried in an Anti-Terrorism Court.

The originator of the speedy courts would taste the medicine he had prescribed for others. It is a great irony because Nawaz Sharif was the most vehement advocate for the so-called swift justice and for the purpose had rushed through legislation establishing these courts. He was even considering setting up military courts, but had postponed the idea because of army's resistance.

Nawaz Sharif had been kept incommunicado since his ouster a month ago. He would be totally unaware of whatever had happend between the fateful evening of October 12 and now. The trial would be a relief for it would end his disconnection with the outside world. He will be able to read newspapers and perhaps allowed watching television. He will be surprised at the change. PTV that had projected him as a saviour would now be showing him as a criminal.

It would indeed surprise Nawaz Sharif that the people have generally welcomed his ouster. Their attitude shows that they care little about democracy and have scant respect for their elected representatives. The same people who three years ago had given him the heaviest of mandate now appear to have turned against him. However, Nawaz Sharif can take heart from the fate of his predecessors. Nearly all of them were dishonoured and had departed in disgrace.

The people are getting less and less tolerant with each succeeding government. For them, it is of secondary importance whether the government is elected or imposed. They want results and want it fast. Two to three years period is the maximum they would give to a government. If in that period they did not see any sign of progress towards their economic improvement, they become impatient and start looking for a change. They hope against hope that the new faces would bring them better economic conditions, more employment and just governance. But nothing of the sort happens.

General Pervaiz Musharraf has inherited a rotten economy and so had Nawaz Sharif before him and Benazir Bhutto before them. It is most unlikely that General Musharraf will succeed where two elected leaders had failed. Short of a miracle—which will not happen—there is no way to turn the economy around. The reasons are obvious and the arithmetic is simple.

Whereas Nawaz Sharif had scared the foreign investors, the present government has forced the local entrepreneur to go underground throwing the economic revival programme into a spin. Sharif's mishandling of the IPPs issue, reneging on sovereign agreements, frequent policy changes, and freezing of foreign currency accounts had brought foreign investment to a standstill. It had also forced some multinationals to liquidate and run for cover. The Bank of America and Mobilink are looking for buyers and so are many other foreign enterprises. General Musharraf will find it an uphill task to restore the confidence of the foreign investor.

The highly publicised drive of the present government to recover the bad loans has raised public expectations sky high. The day of reckoning, November 16, is three days away but according to the newspaper reports, the recovery so far has not gone beyond on per cent of the defaulted amount. The government can forfeit the security, mostly buildings and machinery, imprison the defaulters, but there will be no cash. It would result in double jeopardy. The people will be disillusioned and the economy will further stagnate.

The State Bank has wilfully concealed the fact that the biggest loan defaulter in the country is the country's government,

The industrial and commercial enterprises owned by the state are in default to the tune of Rs. 200 billion, almost equal to the default of the private sector. In addition, the government is in default of Rs. 50 billion to Wapda in unpaid electricity bills and owes hundreds of millions to newspapers against advertising business. How is it possible to revive the economy when the government cannot meet its financial obligations?

Our budget arithmetic discourages prospects of any instant economic revival. We simply cannot generate sufficient development and investment funds because mathematically it is just not possible. We are living beyond our means with no possibility of abandoing this habit in the near future. The major chunk of our budget goes in foreign debt repayments and debt servicing, which is unavoidable. Another major part is earmarked for security, again unavoidable. After meeting these two obligations, there is not much left for development, and investment activities. The people may keep on experimenting with a new government every two or three year, but this problem will remain insoluble.

General Pervaiz Musharraf has proposed to set up think tanks to analyse the issues bewildering the nation and suggest appropriate remedies. When established, their first task should be to analyse and resolve the dilemma of living within our means without compromising the national security.

---

* Courtesy : *The Pakistan Times,* November 15, 1999

40

Reforming the State Economy

** M.S. Qazi*

Shaukat Aziz, the new finance minister is working on the roadmap to put national economy on sound footing. The task is daunting as the economy is ailing and people are in a mood of defiance as well as expectations. The government of the Chief Executive for lack of legitimacy can ill-afford to lose sympathy of people which she temporarily enjoys for deposing the government of a prime minister who in all probability did not have the capability to deliver as his government's performance over past 32 months clearly demonstrated. Enthusiasm and promises of new set up to clear the stable notwithstanding, performance of the new government along with it of the CE will be greatly determined by the people as to how does 'economic factor' in their lives change.

When so much is at stake, reforming the economy should be and is top priority of the government. Spade work is being done and as the press reports indicate the economic reforms agenda is likely to be made public by mid-December. In peculiar Pakistan economic milliueus which are not short on multi-faceted distortions ranging from corruption to poor economic indicators, successful implementation of economic reforms depends upon a number of factors. Most conspieuous and important among them are: economic reforms must be common man oriented as they have suffered the most during current decade of 90s; the reforms must have indigenous inputs and solutions as the IMF perscription has scared the business and trading communities, people are worry of it and finally the reforms must aim at bringing financial discipline vertically as well as horizontally.

The finance minister during his address at the 15the annual general meeting of the Pakistan Society of Development Economists (PSDE), Islamabad on November 05 broadly outlined parameters for economic reforms. He identified spending cuts, documentation of economy, right sizing, privatisation and international donor's support as essential elements for economic reform. No one would dispute about the efficacy of ingredients of economic reforms agenda but it has to be noted that economic reforms agenda would be subjected to intense public scrutiny and its efficacy would by judged as to how quickly it turns around the economy for the benefit of common men and wins the confidence of business and trading community in the country.

Former Chairman CBR was sakes for making a controversial statement regarding implementation of GST across the board inclusive of the services sector. The trading community reacted sharply and their leaders threatened to go on indefinite strike in case GST was re-imposed. The finance minister on November 05 after inaugurating the annnual general meeting of PSDE categorically states that no decision to impose GST across the board and increase POL product prices was taken. Nevertheless this small incident has clearly indicated that public sentiments to accept economic reforms could be negative unless they were broad bases and did not affect those segments of society who till now have reapeded economic benefits in a corrupt system with a large number of distortions.

No one is unaware about the dire straits through which national economy has been passing since past a few years. There are a number of economic problems which the finance minister is to address. They include: low growth rate of economy at 3 percent of GDP against Pakistan's pre-90s growth rate of 6 percent of GDP; current account deficit of approximately $2 bn which must change into positive in next 2-3 years; foreign debt liability of $32 bn; stagnant revenue collection of approximately 10 percent of GDP as against minimum required 18 to 20 percent of GDP, stagnant export at $8 bh over past four years; low rate of national savings and reduced remittances by expatriates and nearly dried foreign investment and so on. These economic issues have to be address with a deep touch of professionalism backed by strong will of the government to implement the reforms and to motivate the people to fully participate in economic recovery. The last element would be achievable only if the economic reforms ultimately would be helpful to the people.

Deconflicting national priorities and IMF demands is equally important. The previous government surrendered inadvertently her economic independent decision making to the IMF officials simply for one reason: she had failed to de-conflict grey areas between IMF demands and national priorities. She did not come up with an outline of comprehensive national priorities in development economics whereby she could be conflict national priorities with IMF conditionalities or implement her own plan to rejuvenate the economy. The previous government like her predecessors worked on adhoc basis out of sheer political expediency which obviously made her more and more dependent on the IMF as the economy kept sliding downward.

IMF prescription to turnaround the economy is well known. But it cannot be implemented in toto unless long and short term national priorities are explicitly stated and the grey areas between national priorities and IMF prescription are de-conflicted. An overview of long and short term priorities is given which are considered essential to define economic reforms agenda.

National priorities for economic reforms have to be laid down within the existing national and international economic environments. The latter would seriously affect national economy through global trading and international financial system. There is no escape from this hard reality. The international financial system asks for three things: Competition, efficiency and openness. Without facting them, Pakistan's economy cannot be an effective instrument to feed and provide services to 150 million people. Presently, Pakistan's economy is way behind on all these three accounts. Pakistani entrepreneurs have to be made aware of the demands of international system and pulled out of a mind set of state protection of low quality products.

Social backwardness of masses because of deliberate efforts in the past by ruling elite not to divert financial resources towords human resource development and concentration of political power and national wealth is selected urban and rural corrupt elite, a recipe for poor governance, is one of the major causes of economic backwardness. Unless the grip of this corrupt elite on state power and national wealth is broken and quantum improvement in the quality of governance takes place, it is unlikely if economic reforms agenda would have a sound footing to change a stagnant economy with a vibrant economic by socially backward people whose ruling elite is proven self-serving and over decades have failed to provide good governance and sound economic development.

It is encouraging to note that the foreign minister recognised failure of governance as one of the causes of economic backwardness. He is reported to have said "Thus for us, it is essential that we take full cognisance of how the failure of governance had translated into our backwardness and what remedial measures would be required to correct such failures and put the development process back on track". It would be watched eagerly how he initiates economic development and links it with good governance in the economic reforms agenda.

The short term priorities are restoring confidence of business community, local as well as foreign. For this resolution of long standing IPPs issues is essential on priority basis. In addition to this following points would need attention while reforming the economy:

Expanding tax net and plugging leakages of tax evasion through gradually improving upon documentation of economy, rationalising taxes and reforming tax collecting administration.

Revitalising agriculture and industrial sector through meaningful incentives and reforms to improve their output.

Reducing debt servicing burden by seeking extension in relief period ending December - 2000.

Improving current account deficit by increasing exports and discouraging non-essential imports.

Maintaining social sector spending at a reasonable level to alleviate poverty and to improve social indicators.

---

* Courtesy : *The Frontier Post (Pakistan),* November 14, 1999

41

Revival of Pakistan's Economy

** Brig (R) Usman Khalid*

It was more than ten years ago that I wrote in an article: "A country where the black economy is bigger than the legitimate economy, stability can only be found under military or mafia rule". I did not realise then that I had stumbled on a fact of such pervasive importance in the politics of South Asia. It explains why Pakistan has had military rule so often while India has avoided it altogether. During the early years after independence, India was led by a political party (Congress Party) with a charismatic leader (Nehru) and a popular base among the working as well the middle classes. It is only after several splits and poor leadership that political mafiosi have been able to challenge Congress leadership. The BJP has its roots in RSS. It heads a coalition govt. of many parties who are diverse in political culture and base of support, but are united by a set of clear national objectives. The Indian armed forces can never match the poltical sophistication of Mafia Rule in India primarily because of the diversity of political cultures that Mafiosi provide a cloak for in the name of democracy.

Pakistan, in contrast, is the name of a dream that has been dreamt by several generations of South Asian Muslims under different names for the revival of Muslim power in South Asia. Since the focus of the aspirations of Pakistanis is the revival of power, it is not surprising that they look upon the strong armed forces as the raison d'etre of Pakistan as well as the principal means for the realisation of their dreams. The rise of ethnic and sectarian parties poses a danger to Pakistan also of being dominated by political Mafiosi.

Moreover, due to the absence of uniting influence of clear national objectives, Mafiosi can cause real havoc as was done by the Awami League in East Pakistan in the sixties. I believe that the coup d'etat of 1999 is different because it followed the old established national political parties (PML and the PPP) being led by persons who ran the country like Mafia land. They made their deals in secrecy and depended on their henchmen and foreign handlers for implementation. Unlike in India, they wantonly ignored the compulsions of national security. Nawaz Sharif was prepared to undermine all the four pillars of our national security—strong and united armed forces; credible nuclear deterrent; Jihad in Kashmir; and Taliban rule in Afghanistan. Benazir is prepared to go even further; she promotes the Advani agenda of undoing the partition of British India.

The Musharraf administration has correctly identified that fighting corruption is its main role and the basis of its legitimacy in power. While the people are generally enthused by the political theatre that characterises accountability; the leadership must know that its serious objectives is to reduce the size of the black economy irreversibly. The tolerance of incompetence and corruption of government officials, the rules and procedures of government business, cuts and commissions in some departments, should all be looked into. It would be necessary to close down many departments that provide no useful service to the public. The departments with entrenched culture of corruption would need to be disbanded and their functions distributed or decentralised. We must not allow return to the past when most departments undermined the very regulatory function they were required to perform and the very sector of the economy they had responsibility to promote.

It needs to be recognised that the primary task entailed in reviving the economy is to put the black economy under pressure and thus promote the legitimate economy. Restoration of party politics until at least 80 percent of the economy begins to work by legitimate rules enforced fairly and impartially, would risk the socio-economic future, even the survival, of Pakistan.

All changes in rules of business of the government have invariably facilitated the black economy and put legitimate business under pressure. The IMF leads the pressure groups for promoting the black economy. Its ways are smart and indirect. While it says its wants the black economy to be crubed, it actually promotes policies that put indigenous businesses under greater pressure. For example, to promote foreign business in Pakistan, it insists on 'documented economy' and 'transparency'. That would help restrain the black economy in a developed country but it would kill business in Pakistan. The large foreign companies used to documentation of all transactions and transparency of company accounts would flourish while small Pakistanis are denied a period of informal transactions they need to build their skills and confidence.

The big foreign companies have other ways of satisfying the demands of corrupt officials, the Pakistanis have to meet the demand for bribes by officials, enforcing a myriad of easily avoidable controls and taxes. The world banking system facilitates corrupt officials, tax evaders, robbers and smugglers with means to transfer money into their overseas accounts. There are procedures and tax exemptions all over the First World where stolen and ill-gotten wealth can be kept in anonymous safety.

Similarly, the conditions imposed by the IMF, ostensibly to stabilise the economy of a Third World country, also favour the corrupt of Pakistan, foreign companies and financial institutions. Every country the IMF comes to assist, is required to allow free exchange of its currency, lower import tariffs, and impose higher taxes on income and condumption. These three consitions combine to create a structural budget deficit and balance of payment deficit that becomes higher and higheras the IMF persists in its help.

The free movement of currency eliminates the costs and enstraints on moving the profits and gains (including that from crime and corruption) across international frontiers. The presence of foreign banks facilitates the laundering of money with the speed of light. The demand for foreign currency is artificially kept high, as the ill-gotten wealth is unlikely to feel safe within the country. The adverse effect is there for all to see. The exchange rate of the Pakistani rupee does not reflect its purchasing power. The rupee has devalued sharply in the international market over the last decade almost entirely because of the demand of foreign currency from smugglers, corrupt businessmen and officials. More recently, even genuine savers have opened foreign currency accounts to protect the value of their savings.

Devaluation makes imports expensive. The IMF, whose charter is to promote international trade, insists that the rates of import duty should be lowered so that foreign imports are maintained at a high level. The effect is a sharp reduction in revenue from import duty. The IMF prescribes increase in taxes on income and consumption (like the GST) to bridge the budget deficit. The taxes are more difficult and more expensive to collect but are easily avoided with the help of corrupt officials in tax-collecting departments. The result is that direct taxes multiply, the tax rates are raise repeatedly, there are howls of protest from the business community, but little additional revenue is raised. The government is forced to borrow money from the IMF or the international banking system. The servicing of the loans becomes an additional burden on the exchequer exacerbating the structural budget and balance of payment deficit.

A country facing such chronic economic problems is not really free as its poor credit rating makes international banking and trade more difficult and more expensive. But too many countries have been so devastated by the IMF in the last two decades. It is now widely believed that the main role of the IMF is keep the economic wellbeing of the non-western countries under so much strain that it is easy to subvert their economies to pressurise them into changing their internal or foreign policy.

In other words, the international financial system is an effective instrument of war. It is pointless arguing if the IMF and WTO have precisely that role. The important things is that they are able to perform the role and the USA has not hesitated to employ its control over the world financial system to twist every foreign arm from time to time.

If the IMF and the world financial system are that powerful, the question arises, is there any point in trying to resist? The answer is, sometimes! The IMF does not interfere in formulation of economic policy of a country that does not seek its help. Most countries can often find an easier way out of their economic problem. When a country is important and is disinclined to go to the IMF, it has to be induced somehow to seek help. The most frequently employed method is to have moles in the finance ministry of the target country and an advisor from the IMF or the World Bank.

Pakistani bureaucrats, often will qualified and competent, have been used in that role all over the world. Naturally, when Pakistan is in need of their services, these are provided promptly and generously. There is such an abundant supply of them that the entire finance team has been supplied from the USA for every administration since Field Marshal Ayub Khan came to power in 1958. The present government has also been supplied its finance team from the USA. But this is neither sinister nor necessarily bad.

The IMF, the World Bank and the WTO are the product of international treaties and can therefore impose policies on countries by overt pressure. Since the effects of the recommended policy are supposed to be benign, one can dispute the measure if the effect produced elsewhere or in ones own country is different. But that would require the members of the finance team, even when supplied from the USA, to be patriotic. If the present finance team were minded to put their considerable experience at the disposal of the government, they would have no difficulty in resisting policies that might jeopardise the economic recovery of Pakistan.

There is no doubt that the present finance team has the capability to achieve the revival of the economy of Pakistan. But, whatever their capability, they would need to be guided by objectives and their performance kept under close scrutiny by the financial press of Pakistan. Let us make a beginning by listing the objectives entailed in reviving the economy. I believe that it was right to start with sorting out the loan and utility bill defaulters and to simultaneously target individual and institutional corruption. The money squandered, embezzled or taken in cuts and commissions needs to be recovered and audit and report system put in place to preclude recurrence.

The people of Pakistan are more keen to see the ill-gotten wealth recovered and would not be satisfied by mere dismissal of the corrupt officials. The recovery of money stolen, embezzled, or taken in bribes, cuts and commissions held in overseas accounts would the crucial test success in which would provide the government with legitimacy as well popularity in the eyes of the people. Fortunately, this is the area where Finance Minister Shaukar Aziz has the most experience and expertise. This would go long way to putting the black economy under pressure but would have little effect in reviving the economy. The indicators of revival would be the balance of payment becoming surplus, the budget deficit narrowing, and most of the 900 factories up and down the country (that ceased production during the last decade) resuming production. The last mentioned is the most important because it is by increased production that we would be able to export more, collect more taxes, and employ more people.

It needs to be recognised that most factory closures occurred in consequence of the actions and decisions of the officials of the government. In many cases, arbitrary exemptions from import restriction or reduction of import duty for a particular person or a particular consignment, was the cause. This was a criminal act designed to defraud the state of import duty and/or to benefit a particular person with large sums of money. It is estimated that 60 percent of the closures resulted from such excesses or demands for bribes by the officials of a plethora of organisation set up for some pointless regulation, minor tax or duty, or control of little consequence. It would be helpful if professionals made the case study of each factory closure. The study should be made public and even printed at public expense. It would be a very useful material for historians researching how our government institutions undermined the industry they were set up to regulate and promote.

There would always be a residual suspicion about the finance team because it has come from the USA. Every time they falter, there would be howls that they are implementing the agenda of the IMF. It is, therefore, important to know what would indicate the IMF agenda being enforced? If the rupee is further devalued, if the import duties are reduced or maintained at present levels, and if the taxation on consumption is moved from the port of entry and factory gate to the retailer, we should know that the IMF agenda is being implemented. If the rupee is revalued, rates of interest come down, import duties are increased, excise duties are merged and rationalised, some direct taxes like the wealth tax that the subject to wanton discretion are abolished, and income tax exemptions (on land owners) are largely abolished, it would be apparent that the finance team is working on a national agenda for economic recovery.

A new situation has since arisen that needs attention. The US had been unable to impose sanctions on Pakistan alone as India had been the first to test nuclear weapons. After the counter-coup in Pakistan, a pro-India Congressman Seven Rothman, has moved a new bill tiled 'Democracy in Pakistan Act of 1999' that would bind the president to impose economic sanctions on Pakistan until he can certify that democracy has been restored. This bill would enable the US to exert pressure on Pakistan while India is spared. Our economic situation could thus be used to undermine the pillars of our security.

While there should be concern that our country is to face harsh economic sanctions, there are indications that the US does recognise that the scale of robbery by politicians had brought

Pakistan close to economic collapse. It is possible the US may co-operate in recovering ill-gotten wealth hidden overseas. But this co-operation may carry a price tag. The US may want early return of Mafiosi in control of Pakistan. That may appear paradoxical but the West always wants to avoid destabilising extremes.

The world banking and financial system can subvert any economy, even prosperous economies. It may not like the system to be unravelled merely to punish a small Third World country. We would need a lot of wisdom and sophistication to make use of this concern to our advantage for the recovery of our economy and improving our security.

---

* Courtesy : *The Frontier Post (Pakistan),* November 24, 1999

42

Recovering Looted National Wealth

* *M.S. Qazi*

The government has many challenges to meet and is to produce tangible results on the seven-point agenda declared by the chief executive on October 17. All the challenges are important if seen in the context of national priorities. However, recovering looted national wealth is the most important challenge, which if met squarely would have number of positive effects ranging from setting pace for revival of the economy to gaining investors confidence to building national confidence and morale. It will also lend credence to the aura of legitimacy to military takeover even if it might be for a limited period.

Looting national wealth, in fact, epitomises all sorts of ills which a ruling elite and their cronies could practise and resort to without any shame and remorse to satisfy their unbridled lust and geed for accumulating wealth. Besides Pakistan, many countries, like Indonesia and the Philippine have suffered on this account. One of the reasons why Pakistan's economy could not turn around despite relief and packages provided by the IMF and heavy foreign loans, has been siphoning billion of rupees out of nationalised banks and financial institutions and through kickbacks on garndiose projects.

Some of the senior executives of nationalised banks and financial institutions were instrumental in the heinous process of siphoning national wealth through dubious and shoddy means. The time, hopefully, has reached when the ruling elite, bankers, industriatists, feudals and other influentials who, if found guilty of looting national wealth, will be punished and looted national wealth will be recovered from them. Unless this is done, it is unlikely if the economy can be put on the right track, investors as well as national confidence and morale and relations with the IMF and World Bank can be restored on sound footing.

Till October 23 when governor, SBP made a public statement in a television programme, there have been various estimates about the amount of outstanding loans. All those estimates have proved incorrect. The amount of looted national wealth is much more and shocking.

According to the governor SBP, defaulters owe Rs. 365 billion. Out of this huge amount, Rs.211 billion is non-performing (loan instalments not paid during past one year) and Rs. 145 billion is defaulted loan (loan instalments not paid for the past more than one year). Rs. 100 billion of defaulted loan is to be paid by 322 families or business groups whereas 100 families or groups owe Rs. 64 billion and their further breakup showed Rs. 30 billion is due from 25 families or groups. These details clearly indicate that major chunk of defaulted and non-performing loan is due from a comparatively small number of defaulters. According to one estimate, there are around half-a-million loan defaulters. Governor SBP has given the target of recovering— approximately 40 percent of the loans—by November 16.

The quantum of outstanding loans is very high. But perhaps, more important than this are legal and procedural intricacies involved in recovering these loans despite firm commitment being made by the CE and governor SBP.

Influential people were granted loans by the banks without judiciously implementing loan-granting procedures and banking laws. It is feared that in most of the cases value of the collateral would be hardly sufficient to meet a substantial percentage of the loan granted. That is why governor SBP during his talk on the television forewarned the defaulters that a monitoring system has been set up to identify other assets of the defaulters. He categorically stated that apart from collaterals, other assets of the defaulters would also be confiscated to recover the loans.

Presently 34 banking courts are working in the country but recovery of loans through them has been extremely slow mainly because the recovery laws were not implemented due to political interference. With the end of political government and CE's commitment to retrieve the looted money a great impediment has been removed. Nevertheless a review of existing laws for expeditious recovery of loans and to punish the defaulters is essential.

Default on loans is not a criminal offence. It gives enough leeway to defaulters to play with legal procedures and the law itself. The defaulters can get stay orders from the courts under the existing laws to save their assets from being auctioned. Other impediments can also be created by the defaulters to stall the auction of their collateral and other assets if they were attached to recover loan. The military government is to take into consideration all these factors which would have direct as well as indirect bearings on the recovery of defaulted loans.

Another pertinent point relates to the national wealth stacked by the defaulters in foreign banks outside the country. There have been authentic news in the national press that around $50-80 billion have been stacked in foreign countries by the elite, industrialists and bureaucrats. Efforts must be made to locate such wealth. The government has already put the names of suspicious people on the exit control list. This is the right action and needs to be pursued further.

The government should also declare loan default a criminal offence punishable with minimum one-year rigorous imprisonment. The measure would compel defaulters to pay back their outstanding loans before the deadline of November 16.

The government has established an accountability cell under

the supervision and control of Lt. Gen. Syed Amjad Hussain, Commander Strategic Command. One of the main tasks of the cell is to oversee recovery of outstanding loans. The authorities concerned feel the need for introducing new banking laws in order to make wilful default of more than one million rupee a non bailable offence. Also, in case a defaulter's collateral is insufficient to other personal assets like house, car, etc. could be attached for the purpose of loan recovery. In case such a law is made and effectively implemented, it would be a step in the right direction.

Accountability Cell/Ehtesab Bureau have an uphill task to accomplish. About half-a-million loan defaulters are to be tracked. Some of them could be wilful defaulters whereas others might have defaulted because of forced economic downturn or genuine closing down of their business. Tracking wilful and non-wilful defaulters would be extremely difficult and sensitive. A lot of care and hard work would be required to sift the wilful from non-wilful defaulters. That is where integrity, professional acumen and honesty of the staff who would be discharging their duties, would play an important role.

The Accountability Cell will gain public credibility only if it is manned by staff whose personal integrity is above board, all defaulters are brought to book irrespective of their political affiliation and personal influence, existing laws are made effective and bank officials with whose connivance national wealth was doled out to defaulters are held accountable.

Recovery of defaulted loans is one of the cornerstones of the military government. Her performance and legitimacy to stay in power in timeless frame, would be curiously judged by the public on this vital account. It is, therefore, necessary that all precautions should be taken to make recovery of loans transparent. In case the government succeeded to recover substantial amount of loans, it would help to improve working relationship with the IMF and the WB, gain public and investor's confidence essentially required to revive the economy.

---

* Courtesy : *The Frontier Post (Pakistan),* November 1, 1999

43

Making the Economy Work For the Poor

* *Tarique Niazi*

Gen. Musharraf has populated his executive with officers who are by and large "honest" and "able." He expects them to work their heart out to turn around the economy that, he believes, now borders on a collapse. To salvage a collapsing economy, howerver, we don't need "workhorses." This is rather a task that has much to do with "vision"—ability to see into the future and help make it happen, or keep it from happening.

What is our vision for the economy? Is it human-centred? Nation-centred? Class-centred? Whatever the claims, the economy is decentred from the human masses, who have long been moving on its margins. As a result, neither the economy works for the majority of the people, nor they work for it. Instead, the economy has degenerated into a "racist enclave" that rewards money and power, and favours classes over masses. Macro-economy in particular is "exclusionary" in nature to which masses count for nothing. It works like a "country club," open only to the rich and the powerful. We often see people with money buy their way to power, and people in power force their way to money. For the class interests of money and power, Pakistan has become a real estate, its resources commodities, and its masses wage slaves. In the process, the rich and the powerful have transformed themselves into "compradore capitalists," who intermediate transactions for "core capitalists" on the shores of Europe and America.

An economy that doesn't have a vision to treat Pakistan better than a real estate, its resources higher than commodities, and its masses kinder than wage slaves is fated to founder. We, indeed, need a "generalship" to steer the economy towards a mass-based, democratic, and humane vision. Such vision won't look for clinkers in human masses to toss them aside; it would rather pick the scrap and work it into steel.

An economic generalship will set in motion the structural remarking of the economy, and not just marginal tinkering that has us live from "selective default" to "selective default." This remaking should subordinate the economy to the needs and aspirations of the masses, three-fourths of whom now live outside of it. As such they have no stakes in the success or failure of the economy. Nor is the economy contingent upon them for its survival or success. These "economic outsiders" have rather bound themselves to the "moral economy" of extended families, successive neighbour-hoods, and small townships.

Moral economy sates the needs and responds to the aspirations of its dependent, quite independently of the so-called "mainstream economy." Their lives remain untouched by its ebb and flow. It does not matter to them if Produce Price Index (PPI) trends up, or Consumer Price Index (CPI) trends down. They are least affected if the rupee gains upon or loses to the dollar. They don't feel the pinch of speculations on their paper money, which may punch a hole in its buying power. Their "exchange market" is governed by a "barter trade" in common counteries, human kindnesses, neighborly sentiments, and fellow feelings for all those who live in and around their orbit of moral economy. Stocked up on these "tradition"—non-material values—of courtesies, kindnesses, neighbourliness, and fellowship, they built themselves an "economic church" to live through the grind of daily life.

They jealously guard this "church" of traditions to keep them solvent for meeting the needs of their daily life. Their "equity market" is therefore very sensitive to "external shocks" that could devalue their stocks in "extended families," "caring neighbourhoods," "feeling townships," and even "honor code." They are averse to modern culture of "atomisation of society" or its post-modern hodge podge of "re-made identities."

"Man" is believed to be the workhorse of the moral economy that puts him above non-man creatures—childern, women, wives. This economy is neither "feminist" nor "equalist." It is rather muscle-bound, which however defers to "admitted failings" in health and strength, such as the sick and the elderly. Yet it defies "claimed superiority" in health and strength that challenges their muscle-bound ego.

An economic turnaround, therefore, hinges on the integration of these tens of millions of "outsiders," who are locked out of the so-called mainstream economy.

When next time Gen. Musharraf hears his economic advisors discourse on the virtues of liquidity, duly irrigated by borrowed aid dollars, he may ask them one simple question: What does this borrowed cash mean to an unemployed youth in Badin, a cowherd in Deh Hardin in Nasirabad, a housewife in Karimabad in the snowcapped mountains of Northern Areas, a child labourer in a machine shop, a school leaver everywhere, a drifter nowhere to go, a dying patient next door, or even a General juggling his checkbook to stay out of default on equity payments for his under-construction house?

It doesn't mean that aid dollars should not be a concern of an indebted economy that we are. The point is to widen this concern to include the "little guy" in it also. An economically unanticipated majority means that cash inflow will continue to be drained by the same "fat cats" that the chief executive is now busy herding to their creditors. If there is no structural opportunity for the unintegrated millions to benefit from the financial resources, then we should not be griping about the hemorrhaging of the banking sector that has sunk $7 billion in the black hole of the default loans. The most interesting feature of this "giveaway" is that no banker is held to account for it; nor the governor of the State Bank who has presided over this loot. There is no Charles Keating here, who was made from a multi-billionaire banker to a window-washer within three years of the Savings and Loan Scandal that rocked the U.S. economy in the eighties. Yet Pakistani bankers are the most anti-poor breed that ever soiled this earth.

Just take the most recent instance of the "get defaulters" operation being worked out under Gen. Musharraf. This operation has disfigured the Agricultural Development Bank's "recovery officers" into "loan sharks." They are now rampaging through the country's farmbelt with wholesale agents at the ready to forcibly buy agricultural produce from small farmers in debt to settle their loans. This is at best a "statutory steal."

To counter such anti-poor biases and anti-poor operations, we need structural changes in the banking sector to create financial opportunities for the less fortunate. Pakistan People's Party (PPP), during its first government (1971-77), did attempt to democratise commercial loaning by biasing it in favour of the less privileged. Prior to the seventies, bank's and their depositor's money was a "treat" to the top 21 families identified by Mahbubul Haq.

Although the PPP government remained cash-strapped for the entire length of its term in the seventies, its bank reforms materialised, a decade after, in the eighties when Pakistan was flooded with the Free World's dollars. About a million household—and I repeat house holds—in the eighties graduated from poverty to become respectable members of middle and upper-middle classes. Some of them were even more successful to become rich and super-rich. Saifur-Rahman, Ishaq Dar, Sheikh Rashid, Islamuddin Sheikh and the likes are the beneficiaries of ZA Bhutto's pro-poor bank reforms.

The crummy behaviour of these "former poor" now may disgust many of us; but their travel from a poor past to present riches owes itself to the PPP's bank reforms. Remember, as Iqbal said, every "miner" has the potential to grow into a (evil) "Kaiser";

once the miner becomes Kaiser, he is, however, no longer the miner we once loved to help. But such possibilities should not stand in our way to a broader economic intergration.

Economic intergration has a political dimension also: national intergration that is so dear to Gen. Musharraf. Economic stakes are so vital to an integrated nation that one of the founding fathers of the US—Hamilton—went so far as to argue for limiting citizenship right to the propertied class. This argument may sound "national Drawinism," or "Hamiltonian illogic." But the broader implication of the argument or the illogic leads to "economic democracy" that sure binds the nations. Our nation is, right now, segregated by "economics."

Sensitive to this segregation, our past leaders pushed "modernisation" in the hope that it would lift us from the hidebound insularities of "biradris," "khels," "tumans," and "tribes," to stitch us together into a seamless nation. But these leaders forgot the unevened impact of modernisation that gave us "Saryabs for Baluchs," "Liyaris for Sindhis," Sohrab Goths for Pakhtuns," and Hyderabad and Karachi for "Muhajir Khels." These divisions were and are still mistaken as ethnic markers of identity. Instead, they are economic markers of ghettoised communities that continue to be shut out of the mainstream economy. The opposite of these "ghettos" is the "gated communities" of Bath Islands, E7s, Gulbergs, and Defences. This "ghettoed" and "gated" living has further accentuated the economic divide, which is now seeded with a range of Che Guveras—from Che Altaf to Che Magsi.

So, to reverse this tide of economic segregation, we need to organise the economy in a way that helps it work for the rich as well as the poor. It is a challenge, not a crisis; yet it needs not just a "general," but a "generalship" to reach and reclaim the last economic frontier for the lost generations of the poor in this country.

---

* Courtesy : *The Frontier Post, (Pakistan),* November 7,1999

44

Feel the Nation's Pulse, COAS!

** Brigadier (R) Usman Khalid*

I resigned from the Pakistan Army in September 1979 in protest against martial law in my country. Twenty years later, I am rushing to Pakistan join the people of my country and dance in the streets with joy at the coup d'etat of 12th of October. I say this with pride that the day of dismissal of Nawaz Sharif government was the happiest day of my life. It is indeed ironical. But it also speaks volumes for the change in the Pakistan Army, its transformation from the colonial army to a national army. It is the first time that the army has removed the civil government in strict compliance of its duty to defend the country. General Ayub Khan took over in 1958 for the reason that frequent changes of civil government were giving Pakistan a bad name. In 1979, General Yahya Khan was handed over a situation when Indian penetration of the body politic of East Pakistan was complete and India had already secured the support of the West for invading East Pakistan to force its secession. General Ziaul Haq took over the reins of government in 1977 to "restore law and order. In all these cases there was a problem of internal security where temporary intervention by the armed forces could have been helpful but long military rule created more problems than it solved. This time the armed forces have intervened to remove a prime minister who was himself subverting the security of the country. Unmindful of his duty to the state and the people of Pakistan, the deposed prime minister was willingly implementing the agenda of our enemies. What makes this intervention so popular and inevitable is the fact that the main opposition leader is even more willing to implement the agenda of Pakistan's enemies.

The 12 October coup d'etat is receiving a lot of attention world-wide and the West has been quick to condemn it. But no publicity is being given to the reasons why it was so vital to safeguard the security of Pakistan. The facts are that Nawaz Sharif was ready to sign the CTBT on 20 October and compromise the nuclear deterrent of Pakistan. He was ready to approve the American plan for the partition of Kashmir before the forthcoming visit of President Clinton to India, Pakistan and Bangladesh. He had already agreed to plans made by the CIA to use the Pakistan Army for operations against the Mujahideen in Pakistan, Kashmir and Afghanistan. The 12 October coup d'etat saved Pakistan from a civil war, secured the nuclear deterrent and Jihad in Kashmir, and avoided our fraternal bonds with the Taliban from being irreparably damaged. That is the reason why the West has been so quick to condemn this coup d'etat. That is why the Americans have unleashed threat of sanctions of all kinds so soon and so brazenly.

The Americans had commanding influence over all the leaders of all political parties of Pakistan. The politicians of all hues have been pliable instruments in the hands of the US; they willingly co-operated with the US to subvert the will of the people of Pakistan. That is why the West in general and the US in particular are so eager to see the politicians put back in power. That is the truth.

Clearly, the US is unhappy. After all, Nawaz Sharif was pursuing the American agenda. The United States cannot escape responsibility for the coup d'etat. It pushed Pakistan to adopt policies and take actions that are clearly against the interest and opposed to the will of the people of Pakistan. It used the IMF as well as sanctions and threats of all kinds in an effort to force

Pakistan to abandon the nuclear deterrent and Jihad in Kashmir and to sacrifice the security of fraternal relations with the Taliban. The army warned the prime minister not to compromise the three vital pillars of the security and survival of Pakistan. He did not only not listen, he used the divide and attack tactics against the army that he had employed successfully against the judiciary and the presidency. Since no political party had pledged the defence of the three pillars of our security, I had argued since the Washington Declaration that there is no way we can secure the vital pillars of our security unless the army intervenes. In the end, Allah (SWT) in His Infinite Mercy, made the overthrow of the evil regime of Nawaz Sharif possible more smoothly and at less cost than any deliberate plan.

There is a lesson in this for the rulers of Pakistan as well as the US. Pakistanis need to learn that the right to leadership is drawn from submitting to the will of the people. Trying to subvert their will is treacherous and evil. America needs to learn that in the pursuit of their transient interest in far-off lands, they should not try to subvert the will of the people by bribing or blackmailing their leaders. If they do so, the ill will they get would outweigh their gains by a wide margin. Particularly, when they practise bribes or blackmail against countries they claim to be friendly with, they support a culture of dirty tricks and subversion with serious implications for the reputation and credibility of politicians throughout the democratic world.

American pressures and dirty tricks have played havoc in many countries notably in Lebanon and Somalia. In the end, these countries survived by giving up on having a government of any shape or form. The Americans infiltrated every shade of the political spectrum, thus acquiring such complete control that all political instruments were discredited and rendered ineffective. Pakistan has reached the same state. The Americans have infiltrated every political party in Pakistan. They are so eager to re-establish them in control that they were putting pressure on General Musharraf within hours of his take-over. We are all familiar with the concept of "religion as the refuge of scoundrels". We are now witnessing the emergence of the institution of "democracy as the refuge of scoundrels".

I have myself campaigned against military rule but I am now convinced that the present military rule has to continue until we can establish a political system that can avoid foreign infiltration and resist enemy pressures. The more the West stresses the need for quick restoration of democracy in Pakistan, the more I am persuaded that return to the old political norms is against the interest of Pakistan. We need to change our political culture so that public service and partriotism are rewarded and corruption and treachery punished. At this moment in time, the army has complete confidence of the people. Benazirs of this world and their foreign patrons would try to dent this confidence. The army would be portrayed as inept and unprepared. There will be western sanctions and condemnation. But this is the classical combination that creates an environment for necessary changes in our political system and culture that we desperately need. We are not scholars or politicians; we are soldiers. Our weapons are integrity, high motivation, and spirit of sacrifice. We will make mistakes, even blunders. But we would resist pressures and learn from our mistakes. We will go forward. Pakistan will become secure and prosperous.

At this time, the military are inundated with advice. Most of it is genuine and much of it quite useful. But at the age of 65, with 28 years of service in the army and twenty years as a journalist, politician and businessman, I have learnt that there are many ways of achieving the same goal. But clear goals and objectives are essential starting point for any successful endeavour. Our national objective today is to resist foreign and internal pressures that threaten our nuclear deterrent, our jihad in Kashmir, and our brotherly relations with the Taliban. The priority of the government should be to reinvigorate the economy of the country, closing avenues for corruption and making honesty and hard work pay. The pressures from the West are a blessing. They are not only helping us know our friends from foes, they are helping us differentiate right from wrong. We need nor fear western sanctions.

We are already under US sanctions, and our needs are simple that can be easily met from elsewhere. For every dollar of western investment that we might lose, we would get ten dollars from extra motivation, hard work and from friends and brothers.

At this time, the army has the support of all the segments of the society. The army needs to be inclusive and ignore the support of no segment because of its past affiliations or actions. But we must not forget that our people have placed their faith in those in uniform. They carry the authority as well as the responsibility. They cannot allow anyone to share power with them by right. Whether it is achieved by promulgation of martial law or by a vote of the National Assembly, General Pervaiz Musharraf would have to be the president and the chief executive. He may take any number of advisors to help him and advisors may similarly assist the provincial governors appointed by him. But the power to make policy and implement vital decision dealing with the security of the country should continue to reside in the military.

The armed forces have a mandate to change the political system to ensure that foreign countries cannot have commanding influence over the political apparatus ever again. Until that is done, no elections can be held. Vital decisions seen to be controversial may be approved by the people directly through a referendum. I am certain the armed forces would continue to enjoy the support of the people as long as they make their priorities their own. The recovery of stolen or rill-gotten wealth particularly that hoarded abroad, is the top priority of the people of Pakistan. We would need the co-operation of the West to secure that objective. I believe we can put them on the defensive by demanding their co-operation against money laundering operations by Pakistanis. After all, Pakistan is a post-imperial nuclear state that threatens no one. Maybe the West may see that its anti-Muslim prejudices are working against their own best interests.

---

* Courtesy : *The Frontier Post (Pakistan)* October 16, 1999

45

The Stepping in of the Army

* *Ras H. Siddiqui*

The news of October 12, 1999 was not too much of a surprise for people of Pakistani origin here in the US. Actually it was the press release the night before that really caught our attention. On Monday night we slept to the report that the military chief of Pakistan, General Pervaiz Musharraf had been dismissed by then Pakistani Prime Minister Nawaz Sharif and replaced by the head of the country's intelligence branch (the ISI), Lt. General Khwaja Ziauddin. That was the real surprise because Pakistan's army chiefs are not the ones usually fired by elected heads of government. Lt. General Ziauddin had recently been in Washington, along with the Pakistani Shahbaz Sharif. The way many Pakistanis saw it, Washington may have given its blessings to the military chief's dismissal as its views have always been important in Islamabad. But as America awoke Tuesday morning, it appeared that the tables had been turned and the elected prime minister was the one out of the job. Now that is something that Pakistanis historically are used to.

The question now is: how does Washington perceive the situation today especially with the news on Thursday that a state of emergency had been declared in Pakistan, the Constitution is to "remain in abeyance" with General Musharraf as "chief executive" (whatever that means) of the country while the Parliament is to remain suspended? And no civilian interim setup has been described something that many observers including this writer, has expected. Now the question is: have the "Young Turks" taken over in spite of Washington's objections?

To delve into a little bit of history, Pakistan especially since 1958 (the year that the military directly intervened to take control under General Ayub Khan) had been America's most "allied ally". It became a significant part of US's anti-Communist crusade in Asia. A military dictator by the name of General Ziual Haq was once the darling of America even after he had overthrown Prime Minister Zulfikar Ali Bhutto (1977) and had him judicially executed (1979).

But in 1990 the Bush Administration formally changed this relationship by stopping all military aid, even spare parts to Pakistan under the country-specific Pressler Amendment to discourage it from going nuclear. Pakistanis often joke that for Pressler to be applicable, the flag of the sanctioned country had to be green, with a white crescent moon and a star on it, and it's language Urdu. As one prominent writer in Pakistan most aptly put it, after the demise of the Soviet Union, helped by its defeat in Afghanistan, the US threw away Pakistan as if it was "a used lemon". Another writer added the Washington's stand during this summer's face-off with India in Kashmir was another grim reminder of that lemon status. So that is where public opinion stands. India's perceived "victory" in the Kargil war against "Pakistani-backed freedom fighters" landed as a huge liability into the lap of Prime Minister Nawaz Sharif.

Sharif projected himself as a "made-in-Pakistan" leader as opposed to his more talented rival, "made-in-the-West" "Daughter of the East" Benazir Bhutto. But then he went to Washington and signed a very unpopular agreement to withdraw military support and personnel from the Kargil area in Kashmir (what was the Clinton Administration thinking?). Not a very good July 4th for Nawaz Sharif as Pakistani perceptions are often much more important than the ground reality. If the Americans want to know the reasons why there are no widespread street demonstrations against the ouster of Nawaz Sharif, his meeting with President Clinton and his agreement to protect the "sanctity" of the LoC in Kashmir may explain some of it.

In essence, the democratically elected leadership with the "heavy mandate" was perceived to have folded on the one issue that Pakistanis can overwhelmingly agree upon. That is that the LoC is unholy and the Kashmir is a disputed territory whose people have yet to decide which country to join as promised to them on more than one occasion by the United Nations. The Washington agreement may have provided the world with a status quo but it succeeded in angering a great many Kashmiries and Pakistanis. The perception was that this was a personal "sell-out" by the elected prime minister (even though he may have been right?).

On another note, Nawaz Sharif was not the perfect democrat. Although generally thought of as a "nice guy" lacking the ego that always got the Bhuttos into trouble, he should have done more to make sure that the Pakistani press was not intimidated. Rehmat Shah Afridi, editor of the *Frontier Post* is still in jail and Najam Sethi of the *Friday Times* was harassed, jailed and released recently, along with others. The deposed prime minister had also been instrumental in removing the former president and had forced out the Supreme Court chief justice. And as one friend put it, if he had only worked as hard on improving the Pakistani economy as he did on discrediting Benazir Bhutto worldwide, he would have much more support today.

Now to American perceptions. The western world led by the United States, appears to be interested in mainly two areas related to Pakistan here. The first is the nuclear capability of Pakistan and the second is fundamentalism. It has already been well established that the Pakistani nuclear programme has always been and still remains the domain of its armed forces and thus this coup has little or no impact on it, as nothing has changed. Fundamentalism, on the other hand, grows in lawlessness and desperation. The continuing anarchy in Afghanistan is one such example. It is amazing what a good job and prospect of a better standard of living will do to defeat the intentions of fascists. Osama bin Laden or the Taliban only come into the picture in Pakistan if the economy there fails.

In concluson, some recommendations: Beyond making statements of "no business as usual" with Pakistan, it would be unwise for Washington and the western economic powers to alienate Gen. Pervaiz Musharraf. Unless the coup leaders do something nasty, it would be better to let things cool there for a while. The US should continue to call for an elected government in Pakistan, because coups should not be accepted as a norm. But President Clinton should go to Pakistan as planned (along with India and Bangladesh) early next year. Regional stability has to be encouraged. And Pakistan still needs to be bailed out economically. Not just by the approval of more loans but also by the permanent retirement of some of its enormous debt. Realistically sanctions will backfire.

On his part General Pervaiz Musharraf will need to make sure that whatever aid does arrive, is used wisely and not lost to corruption. And last but not least, Washington needs to finally do something about Kashmir. Because the road to fundamentalism in Pakistan, which may have once gone through Kabul and Kandhar in Afghanistan with the active participation of the United States, today passes through the miserable lives of the Muslims in Indian-occupied Kashmir.

---

* Courtesy : *The Frontier Post (Pakistan),* October 19, 1999

46

Islam, Democracy and Military Rule

* *Khalid Bin Sayeed*

The Qur'aan makes it clear that Islam is one of the three great universalist religions: In truth hath He sent down to thee the Book, "which confirmeth those which precede it: For He had sent down the Law, and the Evangel aforetime, as man's Guidance; and now hath He sent down the Allumination." (Al-Furkan, 3:3-4)

Islam is based on the worship of one true God who has no equals, no rivals, no children. This is the principle of the Towhid A clear sign of man's worship of one true God is the fact that the prostrates in his prayers before God.

This prostration is due only to God and man cannot prostrate before any other being. Thus this act of prostration makes man independent of everyone except God. Iqbal in his work "The Rod of Moses" expresses the idea graphically when he says, "This prostration that you find difficult or onerous liberates you from thousand prostrations".

Another major component of the seedbed of representative government is zakat (charity tax). This tax in Islam is obligatory and does not represent just charity or kindness towards the poor but the Qur'aan makes it clear that the poor have rights on the incomes of the rich. Zakat is the bedrock of Islamic social justice. It is through zakat that the community is supposed to redistribute income and power among the low-income groups so that they can play an active and equal role with the more wealthy members in the affairs of the community.

A third cardinal principle that can be derived from the Qur'aan is the concept of asking questions. There is the famous chapter entitled Abasa (80: He Frowned). This chapter is a reference to the blind old man who came to see the Prophet when he was engaged in his conversations with certain rich and powerful leaders of the tribes. The following verses reveal what transpired between the Prophet and the blind old man.

> (The Prophet) frowned
>
> And turned away.
>
> Because there came to him
>
> The blind man (interrupting)
>
> But what could tell thee
>
> But that perchance he might
>
> Grow (in spiritual understanding?)
>
> Or that he might receive
>
> Admonition, and the teaching
>
> Might profit him?
>
> As to one who regards
>
> Himself as self-sufficient,
>
> To him dust thou attend. (1-5)

Thus what the Qur'aan is making crystal clear is that every member of the community, no matter how humble he or she is, has a right to ask questions even to the Prophet. And when the Prophet, because of his preoccupations, frowns he is chastised.

All this is a part of the larger doctrine of social equality that Islam advocated and followed and perhaps largely because of this social equality that it spread with such astronomical speed to the adjoining lands of the Middle East and North Africa within one generation. A moving example of this social equality is the sight of the second caliph, Omar, entering the city of Jerusalem as a conqueror leading the camel with his servant sitting on the camel. It was apparent that they had taken turns and it was the turn of his servant to ride the camel with the caliph leading it.

The Qur'aan has to be read in its totality in order to see how women were accorded progressively equal rights. It was well known that the Prophet encouraged women and his wives to play an active role in the affairs of the community and even allowed them to criticise him. It was reported that some of the companions were shocked when they learned that his wives criticised the Prophet from time to time. A very perceptive writer, Karen Armstrong, in her book, "A History of God" refers to the role that women played vis-a-vis the Prophet in persuading him to concede better and equal rights to women. "One of their most important questions was why the Koran addressed men only when women had also made their surrender to God. The result was a revelation that addressed women as well as men and emphasised the absolute moral and spiritual equality of the sexes". (p.158, The History of God).

A forceful indication of how the Qur'aan makes man the architect of social change is when it declares that God does not change the condition of the people until they change what is in their hearts and souls (11:13).

Perhaps the above analysis explains why Iqbal in a letter to Jinnah, dated May 28, 1937, wrote, "For Islam the acceptance of social democracy in some suitable form and consistent with the legal principles of Islam is not a revolution but a return to the original purity of Islam". He contrasted this with the prospect that Hindus in India faced when he wrote, "That if Hinduism accepts social democracy it must necessarily cease to be Hinduism".

The situation that stares us in the face is that despite such dreams based on the hope that Islamic ideas would help Muslims to achieve social democracy have gone awry. Pakistan has spent, since its establishment in 1947, half of its political existence under military domination. How does one explain this striking divergence between ideals and reality? This is because Muslims like others do not often realise that certain declared principles or ideas in the scriptures cannot be translated into practice unless the leaders and other members of the community make a conscious effort to adapt these ideas progressively and perhaps painfully through certain concrete modes of action. Ideas have to be grounded or well anchored in activities.

It is precisely in this regard that Muslims have often failed. They seem to think that just because the Qur'aan makes certain declarations supporting certain ideas or principles that members of the community will automatically translate them into practice. Ideas as they stand are difficult to be implemented. They are sometimes misunderstood. They very often run counter to the interests of certain members of the community. This gap between ideas and their acceptance or implementation can be bridged slowly and patiently. Resistance to such ideas may be overcome sometimes by retreating from them or abandoning them until sustained efforts and creation of public support will enable the community to move towards their progressive acceptance. For all this support in the form of consensus has to be created, opposition to misuderstanding has to be overcome.

While Iqbal was hoping and dreaming in the thirties that the establishment of Pakistan would usher in a regime of social democracy, the cruel facts on the ground were vastly different. Sir Malcolm Darling, an experienced and perceptive British civil servant in India, recorded his findings about the plight of the great majority of Muslim peasants during the thirties and forties. It should be noted that he was describing in his vivid prose the condition of Muslim peasants when the Pakistan movement was being launched. He wrote:

"The peasantry, almost to a man, confess themselves the servants of the one true God and of Muhammed, His Prophet, but in actual fact they are the servants of landlord, money-lander, and pir. All the way down the Indus from far Hazara in the north to Sindh in the south these three dominate men's fortunes; and though they are found in greater or less degree all over the province, nowhere are they so powerful".

What is the way out? Where should Pakistan turn to? The hopes of Iqbal for the setting up of social democracy in Pakistan have disintegrated and Pakistan is following once again the rhythms of military rule with no clear prospect as to when this will end and, above all, what further havoc and setback it will create for the development of Pakistan's political system. It is astonishing that the dominant elites in Pakistan neither pay heed to the vision of Pakistan's intellectual founder, namely Iqbal, nor do they seem to have read with any care the major ideas and principles that their religion, Islam, has put forward and these principles, as we have argued earlier, are in favour of representative government.

As we have seen, these acts of deviance have arisen because either Pakistan's elite have followed the colonial tradition of autocratic government or many of its religious leaders have interpreted Islam in a very rigid and un-imaginative terms.

It has often been forgotten that the Prophet of Isam enjoined his followers to adopt a thoughtful and liberal attitude towards social problems rather than adhering to some narrow interpretation of the Qur'aan and the traditions of the Prophet. The following instructions, which the Prophet gve to H. Mu'adh bin Jabal when he was appointed as an officers serving the government of Janad which was a part of Yemen. This one of the traditions of the Prophet recorded by Tirmidhi states:

"When the Prophet sent Mu'adh b. Jabal to Yemen, he asked, 'By what will you decide a disputed issue?' 'By the Qur'aan', replied H. Mu'adh. 'And if you do not find the required judgement in the Qur'aan', asked the Prophet. 'By the practice (of the Prophet)', said H. Mu'adh. The Prophet again asked, 'If you do not get any guidance from precedent too?' He said, 'I shall then use my personal discretion'. 'Then', said the Prophet, 'God be thanked that He has gifted the messenger of His Messenger with what His own Messenger appreciates dearly." (cited in Allamah Shibli's "Sirat-un-Nabi", Vol II, pp61-62)

The Prophet by asking his messenger to follow his judgement and discretionary power in dealing with difficult social or political problems was following the central ideas and characteristics that the Qur'aan had stated as those of Islamic intellectuals and men of vision. The Qur'aan referred to such individuals as ulu'l-albab (men of understanding). It should be noted that such men of understanding do not have fixed or rigid ideas.

Winston Churchill once remarked, "No one pretends that democracy is perfect or all-wise. Indeed, it has been said that democracy is the worst form of government except all those other forms that have been tried from time to time."

The clear lesson of Pakistan's recent history tells us that the only way Pakistan's leaders can move the country forward towards economic and social change is to create such awareness and consciousness among their common people that they will support their leaders for all such undertakings. Failures of democracy through corruption at the top have obviously created serious obstacles for the political and social development of Pakistan. But when we take into account the problems and setbacks that Pakistan has suffered under military rule, it is not an exaggeration to say that the failures of the military rule may even be greater.

Pakistan and other Muslim societies can derive certain clear lessons both from some of the major principles and ideas of Islam as well as from the evermoving tide of human history. It is obvious that Muslim people, wherever they may be, cannot be forced into following certain hastily devised and selfish interests of their power-intoxicated civil or military elites. Private or sectional interests of the power elites have to be modified and balanced by the social interests of the great majority of the people. Of course, such a profound dialogue or interaction between the leadership and the people can only be brought about through the development of mechanisms like political parties and democratic participation of the people in the affairs of government.

The only way out of the morass the present military rulers of Pakistan are in the process of landing themselves into is to announce a clear commitment that the only objective that these rulers seek is the social and economic well being of the great majority of their common people. Such an announcement by itself is not enough. They have to go on record and state clearly that they propose to accomplish a more than modest well being in the conditions of their people within a certain stated period of two or three years.

---

* Courtesy : *The Frontier Post (Pakistan)*

47

Power and Divine Intent

* *Anwar Ahmad*

Who could have imagined the Sharifs disappearing so suddenly from power? Almost everybody. In fact, far messier scenes than the cordial "countercoup" that finally removed them had since long been the focus of animated tea-stall and drawing room discussions. The firmer they seemed in the saddle, the stronger grew the belief in their shift and sudden fall.

Call it faith in the Almighty's warnings against treading haughtily on His earth. Or superstition, a collective quirk or prescience ingrained by centuries of watching countless crowned heads roll in blood and dust. When a wayfarer stepped on an ancient skull, the crumbling bones admonished him thus:

Khene laga keh dekh kay chal rah bekhabar

Main bhi kabhi kissi ka sar-e-purgha-roor tha

This haunting portrayal by Mir Taqi Mir may mean nothing to the proud heads, but is immense solace to those who suffer at their hands. Thus, no sooner does a ruler ascend the throne, people start searching for signs. The first glimpse of arrogance is seen as the dismantling of the first brick of power.

Few would recollect what Zulfikar Ali Bhutto said on PTV amidst mounting agitation against him. But the image etched on every mind is of a derisive Bhutto thumping the arms of his chair to stress that, while he was weak, this chair was very strong. Within days of this fateful utterance, he was swept from power to become a tragic hero in a horrifying drama. Ever since, the "strong chair" has become a metaphor—a symbol simultaneously of arrogance and weakness, signifying the proximity of doom.

Ziaul Haq took care to present an aura of humility. Only those who crossed his path discovered the ruthlessness beneath the self-effacing, God-fearing image. His protege, Nawaz Sharif, copied the image of piety and was kind and compassionate to individuals. But an inherent insecurity, accentuated by a self-image of nothingness without power, compelled the building around himself of a fort of invincibility. The younger brother prided his shortfused arrogance, and contempt for human dignity.

Together with the patriarch, they launched the heavy mandate on exactly the wrong note. On taking power, one brother said they would rule for 10 years. No, corrected the other, 15 years. To a people who believe that even the next breath is an uncertainty, this was tempting fate—even a downright sacrilege.

Then, in the first open court at Faisalabad, the ex-permier ordered some officials arrested. Their handcuffed images were duly paraded in Khabarnama. Next day's newspapers also splashed to story as the beginning of "on-the-spot justice".

Tucked inside, however, was a damning bit. As he was being dragged away by the police, one luckless man kept pleading innocence and, in desperation, said: "Mian Sahib! Khuda say darain". The shattering power of this helpless cry silenced for a moment the whole pack of wolfish sycophants and the ex-premier. It was to be a fateful moment.

The then chief justice, Sajjad Ali Shah, took suo moto cognizance of the incident. The police lied through their teeth to suggest that the prime ministerial impulse was, in fact, their painstaking doing. Finding the case full of legal flaws, Justice Shah bailed out the officials.

The 'audacity' was taken as an affront by the ex-premier, and the seeds of discord with the judiciary were sown. Then followed a saga that must rank as one of the darkest in our murky history. To save the throne, as the world watched the Supreme Court was brazenly invaded by those who are now invoking democracy and constitutionality. Even worse was to follow. The highest court of our luckless land, before which one bowed on entering and taking leave, was torn as under and, as the nation watched in horror, killed its own credibility.

The twin ouster of Justice Shah (whose constitutional call for help went unheeded by the ex-army chief General Jehangir Karamat) and former president Leghari was a 'triumph' too euphoric to leave room even for pretended humility. Subsequently, when Gen. Karamat also resigned ("for his own reasons", says, Gen. Pervaiz Musharraf), the mandate indeed seemed impregnable.

Ms. Bhutto also chose (for her own reasons, no doubt) to stay abroad after the guilty verdict on corruption charges. Ironically, the Sharif camp has now joined her in calling for free and fair trials. Hopefully, both would have their wishes granted.

The parliament, please recall, had much earlier happily gagged itself and deranged the president (recall also the "safety-valve against martial law" argument for Article 58-2b). To top it all, one Rafiq Tarar was fished out of the family bowl and anointed president—supremely sardonic to see him, stiff upper lip and all, blessing the new dispensation.

For these sins against the nation, lest they forget as they now begin the dirge on the death of democracy, the then allies of the PML are more to blame. The ANP, the MQM and others had supported all three actions. Even the PPP had joined them in the first two. So, while the Sharifs may have been left alone on the burning deck, many others are also guilty of setting the ship on fire before jumping overboard.

Anyway, having bludgeoned all threats to their throne, the Sharifs seemed set to rule forever. That they had lost all their political allies in the process seemed trivial. That even popular support had vanished and, in fact, been replaced by a burning desire for vengeance could simply not be whispered in the royal ear. No courtier was loyal enough to risk bearing bad news.

No wonder, therefore, that the final fateful words were uttered. Days before the fall, the ex-premier had begun proclaiming that power was given to him by Allah for "some purpose" and, "with His Fazl-o-Karam", no "power on earth" could remove him. Emphasis on Allah's entrustment and continuing support could be an ingrained belief, sheer habit (the phrase seemed an instinctive part of every other sentence) or designed to deflect the perception of arrogance—or all three.

In any case, it did not have the desired effect. A power on earth did depose the Sharifs in a matter of hours, in a most unexpected way and in circumstances that seemed within their power to avoid. No wonder Gen. Hameed Gul sees the coup as an act of God to save the country.

So, going by this logic of second guessing divine intentions, what is one to presume? That Allah's trust was abused and His Fazl-o-Karam had forsaken the Sharifs? Who can judge? And now Gen. Musharraf says, "God is on our side because our intentions are very noble".

History is a chronicle of rulers' invocation of divine endorsement, duly certified by court clerics. Yet Allah is specific in separating the rights of man (socio-economic obligations of the privileged to the poor and the rulers to the ruled) from man's obligations to Him (personal piety). The latter is a matter between man and God, inconsequential to society (unless in translates into public good). But a breach of the rights of man is unforgivable.

The Sharifs had closets full of crimes against the poor (including six Umra trips that reported by cost the people Rs. 150 million). Yet they confidently claimed divine support. The contrast was jarring. Whose side could Allah be on—theirs or the plundered people's? Rather than proclaiming it, shouldn't the rulers seek Allah's support in the welfare of His people? That is also good politics.

---

* Courtery : *The Pakistan Times,* November 12, 1999

48

Religion and Pakistani Politics

* *M Faiz Rehman*

The last Sunday's Los Angeles Times had a two-column boxed item on the top of the newspaper's front page about Gen. Musharraf's views on religion and the ban on Quzi Hussain's entry in his home province of NWFP. Such glaring headlines have become a kind of routine in the mainstream US media, whose obsession with Islam and, as a result, with Pakistan is all time high.

Pakistan's close proximity and association with the Taliban and the monumental publicity given to their version of Islam in the West, and the previous regime's hypocritical policies of fanning fundamentalism, gave hostile press a lot more ammunition to sow the seeds of malaise and doubts in their readership.

Gen Musharraf and his team are being observed under a very powerful microscope. His background, the family, and other connections are being dissected vigorously by ever-hungry reporters and ever-curious thinktanks. One such example was Gen Musharraf's picture with his wife and two family dogs, which was splashed in major newspapers here, suggesting the general is not a fundamentalist.

Sunday's news story in the Los Angeles Times made an interesting observation. It said that Pakistan's mark on the scale of Islamic fundamentalism could be gauged by the number of beards in the society. The story, much to the satisfaction of readers, said that since the number of beards in the Pakistani society is still relatively low, it could be inferred that Pakistan is not a fundamentalist society. The paper also noted that out of 23 brigadiers of the army only two wear beards. The fact that Gen Musharraf only sports a mustache and does not wear a beard occupied a prominent place in the Los Angeles Times story. So, as far as the West is concerned, fundamentalism in Pakistan is only 'beard deep'.

I do not believe that Musharraf's statement alluding to Kemalism was made with a plan. In my opinion, it was only a courtesy remark aimed at touching Turkish sentiments and seek Turk support for the new military rule in Pakistan. Nevertheless the statement has been received with warmth and delight in the US press. Pakistan and Turkey share many common bonds; one dubious common denominator between the two nations is the mighty militaries 'two-cent worth' say in governmental affairs.

Kemalism is not exactly about secularism. Secularism is not about being anti-religion. Secularism allows all faiths in a society total freedom. It rather encourages religious activities by giving tax breaks and other facilities. If a Sikh is elected to the US Congress, nobody can stop him from wearing a turban in the House of Representatives. This is his constitutional right. Turkey is not a secular state. It has become largely an anti-religion state. The recent saga of not allowing Merva Kavakci, a US-based Muslim woman who was elected to the Turkish parliament, but was not allowed to take the oath because she wore a hijab is absurd and painful for not only Muslims, but also adherents of all faiths. The Turkish Supreme Court upheld the decision and based it on Kemalism.

I believe we are tailing about two extremes here. Pakistani polity has become too religionised and the Turkish establishment is too anti-religion. As anything, here again the key is moderation, being middle of the road, which is the precise teaching of Islam, a deen of moderation.

It has been proven time again that the people of Pakistan vote on secular lines. Religious leanings have hardly impacted the election outcomes in the country's nascent history. The major political parties have in their fold all kinds of shades of Islam. From the People's Party to the MQM, ANP or the Muslim League, decisions are not made on the basis of one's version of religion. The Jamaat-i-Islami and other religio-political parties have played an important political role. They have a large following. Their leaders are respected for their knowledge of religion and their position on several world issues. Somehow these parties have not been able to transform their following into solid votes. The reasons are for them to search and establish.

The bottomline is that religious politics will not work in Pakistan in the foreseeable future. This fact is evident by the presence of many politicians in major non-religious political parties, who have their early training done either at the Jamaat-i-Islami or other religious groups.

The only politics that has worked in Pakistan in whatever form or shape is secular in nature. The Muslim League, the PPP, and the MQM, are the three largest parties in the suspended National Assembly, which have Muslims from all backgrounds in their fold.

This is the time for our religious leaders to do some soul searching. Jamaat chief Qazi Hussain Ahmed's claims of having a right to form the next government and his myriad of ultimatums do not go well with the masses as well as the intelligentsia, who haven't forgotten Qazi sahib's performance in previous election. These statements only diminish his stature as a serious politician. There will always be people in the country who vote on religious lines, which is true in other democracies as well. But, Pakistani Muslims will never vote en block for religious parties. The diversity and complexity of the Pakistani society will never allow this to happen.

Pakistan is a Muslim society and it will remain so. We have to decide once and for all whether we will keep on dividing it on religious faultlines or will try to come up with a political system that allows all equal participation and not make them aliens in their own country. Religious parties representing only a portion of a certain sect or school of thought should not expect to lead the entire country. The very notion of Maulana Fazlur Rehman leading the country gives nightmares to people, who do not agree with his style and religious beliefs. Politicians, especially religious politicians, should work towards creating an atmosphere in which every citizen has a chance to be productive and not discarded because of a label representing his beliefs. This is the true spirit of Islam.

Throughout Muslim history, especially in Muslim Spain, non-Muslims played a significant role in the development and sustenance of the Muslim empire. This is only possible when one's rights are secured. The religious frenzy created by our leaders to strengthen their hold on their constituency is scary for minorities within Islam let alone the non-Muslims. Over the years, we have marginalised many Pakistanis because of their religious beliefs.

In today's mail, I received a book from a noted US think-tank, RAND. The book based on a study of the US and China was published for the Congress. Something we can learn from it was the list of writers, which included one Muslim, an Indian Christian, an Iranian-American, and others whose religion was not obvious from their names. Can this be possible in Pakistan, the country with over 90 per cent adherents of Islam, the most enlightened religion, which has emphasized tolerance so many times and on so many occasions.

No 'ism' will succeed in Pakistan unless it creates opportunities for the masses. Our western friends who are still in a state of disbelief over an unprecedented welcome accorded to the military government by the masses do not know that governments in Pakistan hardly matter to a layperson. Democracy never translated into good governance or a slightly decent living for the common man. They were jubilant because they think at least an easy breathing space will come along with the military tanks.

Nelson Mandela has this to say on leadership: "I have always endeavored to listen to what each and every person in a discussion had to say before venturing my own opinion. Oftentimes, my own opinion will simply represent a consensus of what I heard in the discussion. I always remember the regent's axiom: 'A leader,' he said, 'is like a shepherd. He stays behind the flock, letting the most nimble go on ahead, whereupon the others follow, not realising that all along they are being directed from behind.'

How about leading from behind, just for once.

---

* Courtesy : *The Pakistan Times,* October 31,1999

49

US Attitude Towards Army Take-Over

* *Mansoor Mamoon*

The Clinton administration was presumably well aware of the recent army take-over in Pakistan much before it actually took place and the circumstances leading to its occurence. In fact, Washington was buzzing with a rumour of a possible military putsch arising out of the intense power tussle between the government of Nawaz Sharif and coup leaders for about a month. Three weeks before the changeover in Pakistan the Clinton administration warned against taking any extra-constitutional measures and strongly pleaded for the continuation of democratic polity and practices. Nawaz Sharif, Pakistan's dismissed Prime Minister, seemingly attempted a pre-emptive strike against the Army Chief General Pervaiz Musharraf and the Chief of General Staff General Mohammed Aziz. In so doing he could not even imagine that it would be aborted and would backfire.

Within minutes of the announcement of his replacement of both the generals the army moved against him with precision speed and toppled his two-and-a-half- year old government. So widespread was the discontent against the ousted Prime Minister that the rank and file of the army responded to a man to overthrow his government. There was no resistance, not even a murmur or protest from the civilians as well. Even National Assembly members belonging to Nawaz Sharif's own party the Pakistan Muslim League (PML) preferred to remain silent. Rather the people, by and large, hailed the army with apparent glee.

The seeds of ths discontent were sown during the battle of Kargil when under the pressure of the Clinton administration, Nawaz Sharif's agreed to pull out troops much to the opposition of the generals conceding a political victory to India capitalising on which the BJP government drummed up support during the recent elections paving the way for its smooth sail and return to power with increased majority. The Pakistan army genuinely felt that they have been badly let down and that the blame of the Kargil fiasco has been laid on them. The army also took advantage of Nawaz Shariff's alienation from the power base and unpopularity with the masses due to his largely autocratic and highhanded rule - his successive ousting of the President of the Republic, the Chief Justice of the Supreme Court and former Chief of Army Staff General Jehangir Karamat, his crackdown on the voices of dissent - political as well as press, his unabashed cronysm, sectarian feuds and violence, economic doldrums and widespread corruption. The army could well understand the mood of the nation and knew full well that they would be welcome as the saviour of the country. It is, therefore, no wonder that over sevently-five percent of the people in Pakistan supported the army take-over.

After tightening his grip over the state of affairs in Pakistan General Pervaiz Musharraf made it amply clear that he would have to set the country's economy right and deal with the massive corruption. He also declared that "real" democracy would be established in Pakistan with provision for the accountability of the politicians and devolution of power to Pakistan's four provinces and that the army would stay "in power as long as it was absolutely necessary "for putting the country on the right track." He did not give any time-frame for the restoration of democracy in Pakistan as well as the completion of the task he has set for his administration. Former chief of the caretaker government in Pakistan and World Bank official Moin Qureishi supporting General Musharraf's stand said that at this stage it would be difficult to give a definite time-table in view of the existing realities in the country. Probably he hinted at the absence of an acceptable leadership as former Prime Minister Benazir Bhutto, now in self-exile in London, stands equally discredited. The Army also does not want to lean towards any political group right at this moment to avoid any possible divide and controversy among the people.

There are indications that General Pervaiz Musharraf is going to stay as the Chief Executive of Pakistan for a much longer time than expected. Revamping the economy and dealing with corruption in a country like Pakistan are not easy tasks. It may take years. But what is of utmost concern to General Musharraf is to deal squarely with Nawaz Sharif before giving up power. Return to civilian rule and restoration of constitution with Nawaz Sharif intact in the field will automatically invite a severe backlash for the coup leaders. The constitution, kept in abeyance, provides for mandatory death sentence for overthrowing the government through extra-constitutional means. The military administration has already started framing serious charges against Nawaz Sharif including the attempt to kill General Musharraf and two hundred other passengers of the PIA flight by refusing it to land at the Karachi airport. If Nawaz meets the fate of late Zulfiqar Ali Bhutto it will not surprise many.

Physical or political liquidation or marginalisation of Nawaz might be necessary for a safe bail-out of the junta from Pakistan's cockpit of power. Islamabad has already brushed aside the criticism of the Commonwealth and suspension of its membership. While European countries and Japan appear to be extra-critical, the Clinton administration has somewhat softened its stand towards the military rulers in Pakistan after its initial outpourings against them. The United States has officially welcomed General Musharraf's unilateral military de-escalation and troops withdrawal from its international border with India as well as his offer of dialogue to diffuse tension between the two countries. President Clinton himself admitted that he was pleased by what he described as "concialatory tone" Pakistan's new military ruler took towards India. The US Ambassador in Islamabad William Milam was more direct and thought that General Musharraf should be given a chance.

He said the United States was heartened by the military ruler's pledge to "usher in real democracy" in Pakistan. The World Bank South Asian regional chief whose organisation is currently negotiating a $ 50 million `badly needed' loan for Pakistan reportedly said it was not the Bank's lookout what type of government a particular country has, but how efficiently and in which sector it uses the loans it receives. The World Bank is largely controlled by the United States and from the Bank's position vis-a-vis the army take-over in Pakistan it can very well be visualised what stand the US will eventually take. The Clinton administration, to quote an observer, has rightly understood that Pakistan cannot be internally isolated nor will imposition of any sanction or moratorium of aid or loan on it effectively work.

Pakistan has strong moorings and connections in the Muslim countries, particularly among the oil-rich Arab nations. Saudi Arabia has already extended its recognition to the new military rulers.

Other Arab and Persian Gulf countries are likely to follow suit. Any attempt to isolate Pakistan by western countries will, in all likelihood, draw the sympathy of the Middle Eastern countries and in its turn tigger a clash of interests between the western democracies and muslim countries. Already a nuclear power, in fact the lone Muslim country to possess nuclear capability, Pakistan might take a more hard-line attitude, assume the leadership of the Islamic world and pose a threat to the west including continued supply of oil via the Persian Gulf. To avoid such a possibility the Clinton administration is likely to opt for what is called in diplomatic jargon "constructive engagement" like the ASEAN countries with regard to army junta in Myanmar. Against this backdrop other development partners of Pakistan like Japan and European countries will also gradually toe the US line.

---

*Courtesy : *The Frontier Post (Pakistan)*, October 31, 1999.